The Quest
for
Political and Spiritual
Liberation

The descending triangle represents Sat-Chit-Ananda.*

The ascending triangle represents the aspiring answer from matter under the form of life, light and love.

The junction of the two — the central square — is the perfect manifestation having at its centre the Avatar of the Supreme — the lotus.

The water — inside the square — represents the multiplicity, the creation.

— The Mother

---

* Existence-Consciousness-Bliss

The Quest
for
Political and Spiritual
Liberation

A Study
in the Thought
of
Sri Aurobindo Ghose

June O'Connor

Rutherford • Madison • Teaneck
Fairleigh Dickinson University Press
London: Associated University Presses

© 1977 by Associated University Presses, Inc.

Associated University Presses, Inc.
Cranbury, New Jersey 08512

Associated University Presses
Magdalen House
136-148 Tooley Street
London SE1, 2TT, England

Library of Congress Cataloging in Publication Data

O'Connor, June.
    The quest for political and spiritual liberation.

    Bibliography: p.
    Includes index.
    1. Ghose, Aurobindo, 1872-1950.   I. Title.
BL1270.G4025   181.'.45 [B]   75-5249
ISBN 0-8386-1734-4

PRINTED IN THE UNITED STATES OF AMERICA

Contents

Preface

The quest for freedom or liberation is at the heart of every revolution occurring today, in Asia, Africa, or in the Americas, in both the social sphere where political and governmental structures are radically challenged and in the spiritual revolution of consciousness where people's values and visions of life are profoundly reoriented.

The life experience and the voluminous thought of Sri Aurobindo Ghose (1872-1950), twentieth-century Indian revolutionary and philosopher, speak to both dimensions of the revolution—the outer expression of our social environment and the inner spirit of our visions and value systems. Because Aurobindo was actively engaged in the political struggle for Indian self-determination in the face of British rule (1905-1910) and became a highly honored yogi during his contemplative life-style at Pondicherry (1910-1950), he provides us with both a historical and a theoretical model inviting serious study in our day. A further value in pursuing Aurobindo's thought rests in the fact that he speaks within himself a living dialogue between the "East" and the "West." In the words of Robert McDermott,

> the dual ideals of a total resurgence of India and the total transformation of man characterized the mature work of Aurobindo Ghose, the political revolutionary of Bengal (1905-10), and of Sri Aurobindo, the mystical Yogi of Pondicherry (1910-50). This complementarity of politics and spirituality typifies Sri Aurobindo's ability to draw diverse strains into a rich and dynamic synthesis: as he combined politics and Yoga, he also combined Western and Indian values. The condi-

tions for this synthesizing ability were created by the highly diverse strains in his personal life.[1]

A look at his personal life will document Aurobindo's immersion in European as well as Indian culture, indicating that he embodies the conversation of East and West within the singleness of his personality and his own personal intellectual history. To enter into the conversation he lived will perhaps encourage the conversation we desire, the conversation between East and West that our time invites and demands.

My central concern here is to disclose the understanding and valuation of freedom or liberation in the political and spiritual essays of Aurobindo Ghose and to analyze the nature of the relationship between these two realms. To that end, the method of approach marking this inquiry is historical-ethical. It is historical insofar as it is an attempt to enter into dialogue with Sri Aurobindo's thought through the posing of certain questions that are designed to uncover his experiences, attitudes, and understandings of freedom (liberty, liberation) in human life. The quest to discover his position with respect to these questions is historical. The method is ethical in the nature of the questions asked. With respect to the later writings of Sri Aurobindo, one might pose a question: is it viable to do an ethical analysis on the writings of a mystic? Are we not dealing with two very different modes of perception and articulation, modes so different that such a method is inapplicable?

My position is that the expression of values is what gives rise to ethical inquiry and that mystics as well as nonmystics reveal values in both word and act. Whether articulating metaphysical convictions regarding persons, the world, history, and transcendence, or whether overtly offering to others recommendations for living, Aurobindo, both as mystic and as political activist, is offering insight into what he deems meaningful and desirable in life, and suggesting a path for others to tread. The questions raised in this study are pertinent to both mystic and activist; they provoke Aurobindo's writings to deliver meaning with respect to the presuppositions and sources of his thought, as well as why and in what specific ways he assigns value to the experience of political and spiritual liberation.

In *Religious Ethics*,[2] James Smurl outlines an ethical methodology that contains three levels of analysis. I have adapted his outline as a framework for this study and from it the following methodological description is derived.

Religious ethics verbalize in symbolic form meanings that emerge from a variety of lived experiences; religious ethics are comprised of *events* intensely experienced, *interpretations* given these experiences, and *recommendations* offered for others to follow. This suggests that at one and the same time attention is due to the event, to the interpreter, and to the suggested action, that is, to the experience, to the ''meaning-maker,''[3] and to the recommended ethical style of life. As Smurl indicates, religious interpreters do not rest content with declared meanings but press on to suggest ways in which behavior can express these meanings. ''In the didactic movement of religious interpretation a way is pointed out, advice is offered, and a particular way of pursuing meaning may be prescribed. This is the function usually designated as ethical.''[4]

Thus the religio-ethical interpretation of life begins with *concrete experience* immersed in the particularity of space and time, then moves on to a *symbolic expression*, which at least partially captures that experience; the symbol gives rise to a more developed and thoughtful *analysis*, which prompts *plans and procedures of action* as ways to continually create the original meanings experienced.[5]

The approach of this inquiry is to follow these three processes as suggested by Smurl. The first step (experience-to-symbolic interpretation) demands that we briefly look at the concrete experiences that detail the history of Aurobindo's life, noting the significant events that marked his educational years, his political period, and his life as a yogi at Pondicherry. This is the intention of chapter 1.[6] The second step (symbol-to-reflective thought) enables us to discern and discuss the metaphysical interpretations Aurobindo discovered and created in the course of these events. This stage in my method is based on the assumption that one cannot appreciate a particular position on a concrete ethical question without acknowledging the metaphysic (or metaethic) behind it. In other words, in order to grasp Aurobindo's thought on the nature and value of freedom it is necessary to ask him his position on the nature and value of the life context in which we find ourselves. It is necessary to reach back into the presuppositions lying behind his freedom prescriptions. Knowing this background enables us not only to understand his thought more fully and more accurately, but also to test the coherence and consistency of his metaethical and ethical convictions. [7]

Therefore chapter 2 attempts to unfold Aurobindo's thought as a response to several precise questions. What are the presuppositions underpinning his political and spiritual thought? This question, metaethical in thrust, will be discussed in summary fashion, based largely upon reliable critical studies that uncover Aurobindo's position with regard to the divine, human life, the world, time, and what is good. Another question pertinent at this point is, what are the sources of his thought? Knowing these will disclose whether Aurobindo's understandings are rooted primarily in a heteronomous source (such as divine revelation) or in an autonomous source (for example, personal intuition), or in some other alternative.

And the third step (reflective thought-to-suggested action) enables us to analyze Aurobindo's philosophy of freedom and the suggestions for behavior that emerge from his thought. Chapter 3 directly enters into the question of political freedom, explicating the many questions implied. Precisely what is freedom or liberation at the political period of Sri Aurobindo's life? What is political freedom at this time? What are the means by which political freedom is to be achieved? Is political freedom an end in itself or is it seen by Aurobindo to be an expendable means to another end? If freedom is a means, what is the end to which it leads? What is spiritual freedom for Aurobindo during this political period of his life? How does he relate political freedom and spiritual freedom both historically, in his life, and theoretically? In chapter 4 these same questions are asked about freedom or liberation during the spiritual period of Aurobindo's life. (What is spiritual freedom at this time? What are the means by which spiritual freedom is to be attained? Is spiritual freedom an end in itself or is it seen by Aurobindo to be a means to a still higher end? If so, what is the end to which spiritual freedom leads? What is political freedom seen to be during this spiritual period of Aurobindo's life? And how does he relate spiritual and political freedom both historically and theoretically?)

Since the question of freedom or liberation touches the personal-individual level of life as well as the social-communal expression, chapter 5 is designed to discuss this connection in Aurobindo's thought: given his understanding of freedom, how does he view the relationship between individual and society?

In these five chapters I am seeking to understand empathetically the thought of Aurobindo, distanced from any real need or desire to make truth and/or value judgments from any particular philosophical position. This is what Smurl calls the position of the "detached-within." [8]

In chapter 6, however, I intend to shift postures by engaging in critical reflections that not only test the coherence between the metaethical perspective and behavioral recommendations, but also allow me to respond to the issues brought to the surface in the expository chapters. Further, this final chapter will provide an opportunity to reflect upon the nature of the relationship between the political sphere and the spiritual sphere in Aurobindo's thought. [9]

Notes

1. "Introduction" to Sri Aurobindo's *The Mind of Light* (New York: E. P. Dutton, 1971), p. 9.

2. *Religious Ethics: A Systems Approach* (Englewood Cliffs, N.J.: Prentice-Hall, 1972).

3. *Ibid.*, p. 5.

4. *Ibid.*, p. 6.

5. See *ibid.*, p. 10, where Smurl likens this threefold process of ethical reflection to the sociological perspective on human behavior described as externalization, objectivization, and internalization.

6. In analyzing his metaphysical position on the reality and value of the world, Beatrice Bruteau also begins with Aurobindo's life, claiming her approach to be the "traditional Indian approach, first studying the man's life and spiritual experience, so far as these can become available to a mind other than his own, then considering his philosophical system as an organized expression of his inner vision." *Worthy Is the World: The Hindu Philosophy of Sri Aurobindo* (Rutherford, N.J.: Fairleigh Dickinson University Press, 1971), p. 17. See also the foreword to V. Madhusudan Reddy's *Sri Aurobindo's Philosophy of Evolution* written by V. K. Gokak (Hyderabad: Institute of Human Study, 1966), p. vii, and Robert A. McDermott, "The Experiential Basis of Sri Aurobindo's Integral Yoga," *Philosophy East and West* 22, no. 1 (January 1972):15-23.

7. In searching for a tool by which to assess each of the stages of an ethic, Smurl is satisfied with the "good story criterion," which "looks to the story itself, and asks about the inner consistency of its elements as related to one another.... We do not ask if a particular notion of man is correct, but only if it is functionally consistent with its teaching about behavior and life processes. For

example, a religious ethic which depicts history as determined and fatalistic, while at the same time portraying man as a self-determining free being, would be considered functionally incoherent on the basis of the good story criterion." *Ibid.*, pp. 17-18.

8. *Ibid.*, p. v. In "Exploring Comparative Religious Ethics," *The Journal of Ecumenical Studies* 10, no. 3 (Summer 1973):553, Roderick Hindery describes this posture as hearing others' views "inside out, on the wavelength of the peoples who assert them. This kind of listening is the task of the history of religious ethics."

9. At this point I see my position shifting from the "detached-within" to a combination of Smurl's "semi-without" and "without" altogether (*Religious Ethics*, p. v). At this point it should be noted that Smurl's schema "process-people-principles" is similar to my statement of ethical method, though not identical. The difference is largely due to two facts: one, that I am explicating questions that remain implicit in his work, and second, that I am limiting this study to the writings of one particular thinker rather than studying an institution or tradition. I am not offering a study on "Hinduism," nor on the Sri Aurobindo Ashram, nor on Auroville; this is a study of the political and spiritual essays of Sri Aurobindo.

Acknowledgments

I wish to thank several persons who have aided me in my research: Roderick Hindery of Temple University for supporting the project from the start and for providing thoughtful and challenging questions throughout its formulation; Beatrice Bruteau, Aurobindo scholar and author for encouraging this effort and for offering penetrating questions that opened within me new levels of understanding; James Smurl of Indiana University, Robert A. McDermott of Baruch College (CUNY), Judith Tyberg of the East-West Cultural Center in Los Angeles, John Raines and Bibhuti Yadav of Temple University, and Santosh Sengupta of Visva-Bharati University for extending themselves candidly and kindly with criticisms, suggestions, reflections, and recommendations; Jeffrey Russell, Francis Cook, and Douglas Parrott, colleagues at the University of California, Riverside, with whom scholarly discussion is always forthright and fruitful; James Strodtbeck, Gary Jordan, and James Crowell for able research assistance; the Senate Committee on Research at the University of California, Riverside, for support funds.

I thank also Harry Hood, best friend, critic, and husband, for nourishing and sharing the spirit of inquiry and for his understanding presence. I thank Philip and Eva O'Connor, friends and parents, whose lives continue to impress me with their desire and willingness to learn. Grateful acknowledgment is also extended to the Sri Aurobindo Ashram Trust in Pondicherry, India, for permission to quote from Sri Aurobindo's writings.

The Quest
for
Political and Spiritual
Liberation

1

Aurobindo Ghose: Political Revolutionary and Mystical Yogi

Aurobindo Ghose, born in Calcutta on August 15, 1872, was the son of a civil surgeon, Dr. Krishnadhan Ghose, one of the first Indians to be educated in England. Aurobindo remarks that his father "returned entirely anglicised in habits, ideas and ideals"[1] and that he esteemed, absorbed, and endorsed Western rationalism and atheistic thought patterns as well as Western manners and education so highly that he determined that his children receive a wholly European training. In 1877, when he was five, Aurobindo and his brothers were enrolled at an Irish nuns' school in Darjeeling, India; in 1879 the three sons were taken to England to study. While they were living with the Drewett family in England, Krishnadhan Ghose gave strict instructions that his sons be exposed to nothing Indian, whether customs, thought, or friendships.[2] Aurobindo comments on this framework that shaped his early education: "These instructions were carried out to the letter and Aurobindo grew up in entire ignorance of India, her people, her religion and her culture."[3]

In 1884 Aurobindo attended St. Paul's School in London and in 1890 Kings College, Cambridge, where he mastered Greek, Latin, English, and French, and acquired familiarity with German and Italian. Because he had no interest in pursuing an academic career, Aurobindo chose not to apply for a degree.

During his stay in England, Aurobindo received word through his father's letters that a period of upheaval was occurring in India, that Indians were being maltreated by Englishmen, and that great revolutionary changes were on the horizon. By the time he attended Cambridge, Aurobindo had made a firm decision that he would play a decisive role in the liberation of India and he became involved in delivering revolutionary speeches at the college.

This revolutionary inclination was sharpened with Aurobindo's interest in the "Lotus and Dagger" movement, an unsuccessful attempt of Indian students in London to organize and vow to work for the liberation of India. During his first years in India, however, Aurobindo refrained from direct political activity except for a few articles published in *Indu Prakash*, where he attacked the mendicant policy of the congress, its moderate leadership, and its petitionary approach toward Britain, which he felt simply deepened the Indian attitude of servility. It was not until 1902-1903 that Aurobindo's revolutionary tendencies were given fuller expression as he began mobilizing secret societies in Bengal.

Immediately after leaving England in 1893, Aurobindo became involved in the Baroda Service and awakened to a "will for renationalisation—which came, after reaching India, by natural attraction to Indian culture and ways of life and a temperamental feeling and preference for all that was Indian."[4] Baroda was the capital of a small Indian state in Gujarat. Working under Prince Maharajah Sayoji Rao Gaekwar, Aurobindo functioned in the Revenue Settlement Department and the Stamps and Revenue Department. During this time he became absorbed in the study of Indian languages, history, and culture, and soon became more and more involved in education where he learned Sanskrit, Marathi, Gujarati, and Bengali, plumbed the riches of India's literature and cultural heritage, and wrote poetry. He also assumed a variety of educational roles at Baroda College: lecturer in French, Professor of English, Vice-Principal, and Acting Principal.[5]

In 1906 Aurobindo left Baroda to join the political movement, since agitation had begun in reaction to the partition of Bengal (1905). At this point it is important to note the socio-politico-historical forces that brought about this decisive event, for the partition of 1905 served as a springboard to what later developed as the Indian liberation movement, in which Aurobindo played a major role.

Mukherjee and Mukherjee observe that the partition of Bengal (1905) began as an apparently administrative redesignation of boundaries. For the Bengali people, however, it quickly gained the proportions of being a British design to divide them and to rupture their cohesiveness by separating the Hindus and Muslims who composed the population nearly equally.[6]

Bengal had been the largest and most populous province of the nineteenth century with a land area of 190,000 square miles and a population exceeding 78 million people. Under the new partition this would be reduced to 67 million people and the districts of Mymensingh, Dacca, and the Chittagong Division would be transferred to Assam, which itself had been separated in 1874.[7]

The governmental reasons for creating the partition were articulated: to point out the need for administrative efficiency in Bengal, which was becoming increasingly unwieldy in size; to honor the Muslims, who had retreated out of a reluctance to accept Western influence; and to suggest the possibility of granting Assam access to the sea.[8]

The people, however, were infuriated by what they perceived as an attack on the movement of Bengali nationalism, which had continued to gain momentum ever since the foundation of the Indian National Congress in 1885. The financial burden imposed by partition loomed large, as did an attachment to Calcutta, which could not easily be transferred to Dacca. They feared that partition would reignite Hindu-Muslim antipathy since East Bengal and Assam would become a Mohammedan province. In a word, from the people's point of view, it seemed far better to redesign the governmental structure than to redesign the boundaries of the province.[9]

When the partition proposals were publicized, stating that the change would take effect October 16, 1905, the Bengali people reacted with an immediate protest. This in turn provoked them to mobilize for rebellion. In 1906 at the Indian National Congress in session at Calcutta, independence became the newly declared political goal of India. Yet Aurobindo saw the congress president, Dadabhai Naoroji, as dangerously ambiguous in trying to win both moderates and extremists toward a single platform. According to Aurobindo, Naoroji "had actually tried to capture the name of Swaraj, the Extremists' term for independence" for "colonial self-government." Fearing that they would endorse self-government under British rule, Aurobindo fought for total independence.[10]

In 1907 the Congress session at Surat occasioned an explicit split between moderates and nationalists. The nationalists on the one hand insisted on carrying out the Calcutta resolutions of swadeshi, boycott, national education, and complete independence. The moderates on the other hand fought this movement (even physically) and finally suspended the Congress in order to replace it with a national conference with a constitution protecting their party. The split was abysmal and the Congress ceased to exist.[11]

During the Swadeshi movement the slogan "Bande Mataram," ("Hail to the Mother") had become the battle cry of a newly emerging India. This slogan now became the title of an English daily founded by Bepin Pal and continued by Aurobindo. Published in August 1906 through October 1908 under Aurobindo's leadership, *Bande Mataram* became a voice for the emerging party of Extremists, espousing such policies as noncooperation, passive resistance, swadeshi, boycott, and national education; it was unquestionably a key political tool in raising a revolutionary consciousness among Indians.[12]

According to Haridas and Uma Mukherjee, the *Bande Mataram* functioned in two significant ways. First it "opened a new phase in the history of Indian Nationalism" by upholding swaraj or self-rule as the means for attaining freedom, thereby challenging and making obsolete the mendicant policies that the National Congress had been espousing.[13] Second, *Bande Mataram* was designed to reveal the "autocracy of the alien Government."[14]

Aurobindo was convinced that ventilating grievances was an inadequate response to the repressive measures of Britain. He wanted the Congress to be an agent of radical change. It was his collaboration with Bepin Pal in contributing to *Bande Mataram* that prompted him to become a public and prominent leader of the Nationalist Party. Reflecting on these days of his political career, Aurobindo later wrote of himself:

Sri Aurobindo's first preoccupation was to declare openly for complete and absolute independence as the aim of political action in India and to insist on this persistently in the pages of the journal; he was the first politician in India who had the courage to do this in public and he was immediately successful. The party took up the word Swaraj to express its own ideal of independence and it soon spread everywhere; but it was taken up as the ideal of the Congress much later on at the Karachi session of that body when it had been reconstructed and renovated under Nationalist leadership. The journal declared and developed a new political programme for the country as the programme of the Nationalist party, non-cooperation, passive resistance, Swadeshi, Boycott, national education, settlement of disputes in law by popular arbitration and other items of Sri Aurobindo's plan. Sri Aurobindo published in the paper a series of articles on passive resistance, another developing a political philosophy of revolution and wrote many leaders aimed at destroying the shibboleths and superstitions of the Moderate Party, such as the belief in British justice and benefits bestowed by foreign government in India, faith in British law courts and in the adequacy of the education given in schools and universities in India and stressed more strongly and persistently than had been done the emasculation, stagnation or slow progress, poverty, economic dependence, absence of a rich industrial activity and all other evil results of a foreign government; he insisted especially that even if an alien rule were benevolent and beneficent, that could not be a substitute for a free and healthy national life.[15]

Bhavani Mandir, a pamphlet written in 1903 by Aurobindo, was intended to train people for revolutionary preparation of the country.[16] And his 1906 contributions to the Bengali weekly *Yugantar* clearly conveyed his message of open revolt, the absolute refusal of British rule, and even instructions for guerrilla warfare.[17] For Aurobindo believed that a nation has an inherent right to freedom and is entitled to gain that freedom through violence if necessary. His assessment of violent means rested on pragmatic, not on ethical considerations. Unlike Gandhi, for example, but much like Tilak, he never esteemed ahimsa as a universal principle.[18]

Although Aurobindo never took direct part in arms-training, bomb-making, or collection of the ammunition, he was a key inspiration to those who did involve themselves in these tasks, and he retained close contact with revolutionary groups up until the end of his political career in 1910. Though his idea of mass armed revolt was never given expression, he continued to nourish its value and possibility.[19]

Aurobindo was, however, a striking influence on the boycott movement aimed at the eventual overthrow of British exploitation. As a strategy, boycott was pregnant with possibilities: it could be a damaging force for economic investments held by the British, as well as a tool for sharpening the awareness and evoking the enthusiasm of the Indian spirit of rebellion. Of its nature the boycott led to swadeshi, the manufacturing of needed goods by Indians themselves. Refusal to Britain meant productivity by and for India.

In sum, there were three dimensions to Aurobindo's political thought and involvement: revolutionary inclinations, which prompted him to work in secret societies for the goal of armed insurrection; public propaganda, designed to raise the level of consciousness among Indians and to motivate them to commit themselves to independence as an ideal; and organization of the people to oppose and undermine foreign rule through noncooperation and passive resistance.[20]

Concurrently with his intense political activity, Aurobindo deeply experienced the riches of the spiritual dimension of life. He had begun the practice of yoga while in Baroda in about 1904,[21] and he continued to progress in this throughout his political career. Feeling the need to consult an authority on yoga, Aurobindo met with Vishnu Bhaskar Lele of Gwalior in Baroda in 1908. Aurobindo, again writing in the third person, describes their exchange and his own feelings about yoga:

> What Lele asked him was whether he could surrender himself entirely to the Inner Guide within him and move as it moved him; if so he needed no instructions from Lele or anybody else. This Sri Aurobindo accepted and made that his rule of sadhana and of life. Before he met Lele, Sri Aurobindo had some spiritual experiences, but that was before he knew anything about Yoga or even what Yoga was,—e.g., a vast calm which descended upon him at the moment when he stepped first on Indian soil after his long absence, in fact with his first step on the Apollo Bunder in Bombay: (this calm surrounded him and remained for long months afterwards); the realisation of the vacant Infinite while walking on the ridge of the Takhti-Suleman in Kashmir; the living presence of Kali in a shrine on the banks of the Narmada; the

vision of the Godhead surging up from within when in danger of a carriage accident in Baroda in the first year of his stay, etc. But these were inner experiences coming of themselves and with a sudden unexpectedness, not part of Sadhana. He started Yoga by himself without a Guru, getting the rule from a friend, a disciple of Brahmananda of Ganga Math; it was confined at first to assiduous practice of *prānāyāma* (at one time for 6 hours or more a day). There was no conflict or wavering between Yoga and politics; when he started Yoga, he carried on both without any idea of opposition between them.[22]

Worth noting here is the notion of surrender, which becomes central in the development of his yoga later on. Also of note is the final sentence of this excerpt; Aurobindo feels no conflict, no wavering, no opposition between yoga and politics. Both find expression in his life at this time and, throughout his speeches, Aurobindo underscored the primacy of nationalism not only as a political ideal but also as a religion in itself. He believed and preached that India had a mission to the world and that such a mission had to begin with India's own sense of freedom. Swaraj would demand service and sacrifice, self-help and swadeshi. These sentiments characterize the central thrust of Aurobindo's political and spiritual convictions evident in his writings and speeches.

As the Indian spirit of nationalism gained momentum, the British spirit of repression, intimidation, and even terror became more and more keenly felt. Bengal was a likely site for such pressures since Bengal had been the source of agitation ever since the partition. These measures were the occasion for what came to be known as the Alipore Bomb Conspiracy. Two youths attempted to assassinate the District Judge of Muzaffarpur, Mr. Kingsford, on April 30, 1908. Although the plan failed in that the bomb was misdirected and never touched Kingsford, the government interpreted this event as an opportune moment for further constraints against anyone involved in revolutionary political action. This included Aurobindo, who was arrested May 2, 1908; during investigation and trial he spent a year in the Alipore jail.[23]

Aurobindo describes the experience of jail, the acquittal, and his deepening appreciation for yoga at this time:

At first he was lodged for some time in a solitary cell, but afterwards transferred to a large section of the jail where he lived in one huge room with the other prisoners in the case; subsequently, after the assassination of the approver in the jail, all the prisoners were confined in contiguous but separate cells and met only in the court or in the daily exercise where they could not speak to each other. It was in the second period that Sri Aurobindo made the acquaintance of most of his fellow accused. In the jail he spent almost all his time in reading the Gita and the Upanishads and in intensive meditation and the practice of Yoga. This he pursued even in the second interval when he had no opportunity of being alone and had to accustom himself to meditation amid general talk and laughter, the playing of games and much noise and disturbance; in the first and third periods he had full opportunity and used it to the full. In the Sessions Court the accused were confined in a large prisoner's cage and here during the whole day he remained absorbed in his meditation, attending little to the trial and hardly listening to the evidence. C. R. Das, one of his Nationalist collaborators and a famous lawyer, had put aside his large practice and devoted himself for months to the defence of Sri Aurobindo, who left the case entirely to him and troubled no more about it; for he had been assured from within and knew that he would be acquitted. During this period his view of life was radically changed; he had taken up Yoga with the original idea of acquiring spiritual force and energy and divine guidance for his work in life. But now the inner spiritual life and realisation which had continually been increasing in magnitude and universality and assuming a larger place took him up entirely and his work became a part and result of it and besides far exceeded the service and liberation of the country and fixed itself in an aim, previously only glimpsed, which was world-wide in its bearing and concerned with the whole future of humanity.[24]

This passage gives a glimpse of the direction that Aurobindo's life took. After emerging from jail, he discovered a wholly new tone to the political tenor of the country. Although "most of the Nationalist leaders were in jail or in self-imposed exile and there was a general discouragement and depression ... he determined to continue the struggle"[25] by holding weekly meetings in Calcutta and by continuing to speak publicly. It was at this time that Aurobindo delivered his Uttarpara speech in which for the first time he publicly told of his spiritual experiences and yoga. He also began the weeklies *Karmayogin* in English and *Dharma* in Bengali, and participated in the Provincial Conference at Barisal (1909). It was at this time too that he pressed for the possibility of newly formed associations to send their own delegates, thereby hoping to enable the nationalists to attend the all-India session. This became impossible and Aurobindo reconsidered the possibility of a home-rule movement that the government could not repress. Such a movement would clearly be a compromise to leaders such as Aurobindo, for whom the slogan "no compromise" was central. He also considered the possibility and desirability of a passive resistance movement. "He saw, however, that he himself could not be the leader of such a movement."[26] Why not? Perhaps the answer to that question rests within his continued autobiographical commentary:

> At no time did he consent to have anything to do with the sham Reforms which were all the Government at that period cared to offer. He held up always the slogan of "no compromise" or, as he now put it in his Open Letter to his countrymen published in the *Karmayogin*, "no co-operation without control." It was only if real political, administrative and financial control were given to popular ministers in an elected Assembly that he would have anything to do with offers from the British Government.[27]

Meanwhile the government's restrictive policy included the intent to remove Aurobindo from the political scene altogether by deporting him. Informed of this by Sister Nivedita,[28] Aurobindo anticipated their action by publishing an article in *Karmayogin*, signed by him, on the deportation project, leaving for his country "what he called his last will and testament,"[29] confident that this would kill the deportation scheme. He was right. Other measures such as governmental search and arrest were threateningly imminent when Aurobindo "received a sudden command from above to go to Chandernagore in French India."

> He obeyed the command at once, for it was now his rule to move only as he was moved by the divine guidance and never to resist and depart from it; he did not stay to consult with anyone, but in ten minutes was at the river *ghāt* and in a boat plying on the Ganges; in a few hours he was at Chandernagore where he went into secret residence. He sent a message to Sister Nivedita asking her to take up the editing of the *Karmayogin* in his absence. This was the end of his active connection with his two journals. At Chandernagore he plunged entirely into

solitary meditation and ceased all other activity. Then there came to him a call to proceed to Pondicherry. A boat manned by some young revolutionaries of Uttarpara took him to Calcutta; there he boarded the *Dupleix* and reached Pondicherry on April 4, 1910.[30]

It was during his life at Pondicherry, 1910-1950, that Aurobindo was to devote himself ever more fully to the life of a yogi and articulate the spiritual vision of human life and meaning that deepened in the course of these four decades. At one point he writes that his experience of yoga delighted him precisely because he discovered its harmony with, rather than antagonism toward the sphere of political action.

> I had thought that a Yoga which required me to give up the world was not for me. I had to liberate my country. I took to it seriously when I learnt that the same Tapasya which one does to get away from the world can be turned into action. I learnt that Yoga gives power, and I thought why the devil should I not get the power and use it to liberate my country?[31]

Upon his stay at Pondicherry, however, Aurobindo found his yoga becoming more and more absorbing of his interest and energy, and this prompted him to retire from political activity, to decline requests to preside at the restored Congress sessions, and to refrain from any speeches or articles unconnected with his spiritual activities. Because his inner vision assured him that India would indeed gain independence, the need for armed insurrection became obsolete. Although the British Government and a number of Indians themselves suspected that Aurobindo was secretly engaged in revolutionary activities under the guise of a spiritual seeking, Aurobindo states unequivocally that his retirement from the political sphere was total, as was his personal retirement to solitude in 1910.[32]

At the same time Aurobindo insists that his yoga did not empty him of a keen interest in the future of India and the world.

> It could not mean that, for the very principle of his Yoga was not only to realise the Divine and attain to a complete spiritual consciousness, but also to take all life and all world activity into the scope of this spiritual consciousness and action and to base life on the Spirit and give it a spiritual meaning.[33]

It was precisely from a base of spiritual strength that Aurobindo understood himself to be participating in the life of India and the world, using his supramental powers and forces in constant action upon the world. No other kind of action seemed necessary, or more fruitful, except on two occasions. First, he began to intervene when it appeared that Hitler would destroy any forces that opposed him and that Nazism would dominate the world. Publicly, Aurobindo declared his loyalties and sympathies to be with the Allies, contributed to fund requests, and encouraged others to share in the war effort. Inwardly as well, he directed his spiritual force with the Allies, because for him

> behind Hitler and Nazism were dark Asuric forces and... their success would mean the enslavement of mankind to the tyranny of evil, and a set-back to the course of evolution and especially to the spiritual evolution of mankind: it would lead also to the enslavement not only of Europe but of Asia, and in it of India, an enslavement far more terrible than any this country had ever endured, and the undoing of all the work that had been done for her liberation.[34]

Second, Aurobindo participated in the political situation of world affairs in 1942 in publicly endorsing the Cripps offer,[35] because he felt that "by its acceptance India and Britain could stand united against the Asuric forces and the solution of Cripps could be used as a step towards independence."[36] When negotiations failed, Aurobindo resumed his reliance on appealing to his spiritual power and force alone.[37]

Although many hopes and invitations to reengage him in politics were extended to Aurobindo, he consistently refused to return. In 1920 he was requested to become editor of a new Bombay nationalist journal. Bengal pressed him to return to a leadership position. Many hoped that he would join forces with Mahatma Gandhi when Gandhi's campaign was launched. The congress awaited his word. But he would not return, convinced that the work he was doing included but also extended beyond specific political projects.

An adequate history of this spiritual period of Aurobindo's life is difficult to detail, since much of his time was spent alone, away from public observation. Aurobindo seemed not to have regretted this. On the contrary he made it quite clear to his biographers that their task was a difficult one: "neither you nor anyone else knows anything at all of my life; it has not been on the surface for men to see."[38]

However, there are a few well-recognized and significant events that mark this phase of his life. In 1910, for example, Paul Richard of France visited Pondicherry and, upon meeting Aurobindo, grew to be a friend and admirer. His wife, Mira, later met Aurobindo in 1914 and immediately felt with him a sense of identity, rooted in their shared interest in spiritual seeking. Paul proposed that they begin a philosophical review, which he offered to fund. The review, known as *Arya*, was founded to address the highest problems of existence in a systematic way and to synthesize the knowledge of both East and West, unifying intellectual, scientific, and intuitive discoveries. Although Paul and Mira Richard and others contributed to the journal, the central spirit of the magazine was that of Sri Aurobindo, who wrote several series known now as *The Life Divine, Synthesis of Yoga, Essays on the Gita, The Secret of the Vedas, The Ideal of Human Unity, A Defence of Indian Culture,* and *The Psychology of Social Development (The Human Cycle).*

The Richards returned to France in 1915 when Paul was summoned to military service. Mira Richard returned to Pondicherry in 1920, perceived and accepted by Aurobindo as the "Mother."[39] She lived at Pondicherry in the Sri Aurobindo Ashram until her death, November 17, 1973. During the early part of the 1920s, Aurobindo received many visitors and numerous requests for more active work involvement. Gradually, however, he became more and more retiring and the Mother took care of visitors and organizational details.

On November 24, 1926, Aurobindo experienced *siddhi* or freedom of the soul. This is known as the day of victory, and for Aurobindo was the moment he experienced the descent of the Overmind into the physical, leading to the ultimate descent of the Supermind. Aurobindo then focused on supramental truths while the Mother opened the household as an ashram, which is still functioning. On August 15, 1947, Aurobindo celebrated the anniversary of his own birth and the birth of Indian independence. On December 5, 1950, he died.[40]

Review

With this overview of Sri Aurobindo's educational years, political period, and life as a yogi at Pondicherry, the picture presented will serve as both point of departure and continuing context for the discussions to follow.

Experience-to-symbolic interpretation, symbolic interpretation-to-reflective thought, reflective thought-to-suggested action as the three phases of ethical reflection indicate the necessity of understanding Aurobindo's conceptual thought within a dialectical interaction with his life experience, the prompter of that thought. In its description of the major visible events of Aurobindo's life, this first chapter has alerted us to several themes of great importance. To the extent that these themes capture key moments in Aurobindo's life experience and lead to the systematic development of his thought, they can be designated symbols. These symbols are: the thorough immersion in Western thought brought about by spending his educational years in England; subsequent discovery of and love for the riches of Hinduism; revolutionary involvement epitomized in the slogans ''no compromise'' and ''no cooperation without control''; the practice of yoga together with the solitude afforded him in the Alipore jail, both followed by the ''command from above'' to go to Chandernagore and eventually to Pondicherry, leaving political participation to be a part of his past; the meeting with the Mother and the publication of *Arya*; the day of *siddhi* or freedom of the soul, manifesting the descent of the overmind and opening the way to the descent of the supermind.

In the next chapter, attention will be given to the way in which Aurobindo developed and articulated his metaphysical world view, affording us a fuller understanding of what these moments symbolized to him. What is his position on human life, the world, time, the divine, the good? And what sources function as fundamental to the formation of his thought?

Notes

1. Sri Aurobindo, *On Himself*, vol. 26 of the Sri Aurobindo Birth Centenary Library (30 vols; Pondicherry: Sri Aurobindo Ashram, 1972): 1. Unless otherwise indicated, quotations from Aurobindo are taken from the Centenary edition. (Vol. 4 of the Centenary Library [*Writings in Bengali*] contains Sri Aurobindo's original Bengali writings; quotations from this portion of his work are taken from translations available in the *Sri Aurobindo Mandir Annual*, nos. 26 [August 15, 1967] and 27 [August 15, 1968].)

Much of the material in this chapter is taken directly from *On Himself*. However, many good biographies and biographical writings are also available as helpful resources for a historical perspective on Sri Aurobindo's life. See Ranganath Ramachandra Diwakar, *Mahayogi Sri Aurobindo: Life, Sadhana and Teachings of Sri Aurobindo*, 3rd rev. enl. ed. (Bombay: Bharatiya vidya bhavan, 1962); K. R. Srinivasa Iyengar, *Sri Aurobindo A Biography and a History*, 3rd rev. enl. ed. 2 vols. (Pondicherry: Sri Aurobindo International Centre of Education, 1972); Keshavmurti, *Sri Aurobindo: The Hope of Man* (Pondicherry: Dipti Publications, 1969); Sisirkumar Mitra, *The Liberator: Sri Aurobindo, India and the World*, rev. ed. (Bombay: Jaico Publishing House, 1970); S. Mitra, *Sri Aurobindo* (New Delhi: Indian Book Company, 1972); S. Mitra, *Sri Aurobindo and Indian Freedom* (Madras: Sri Aurobindo Library, 1948); Ambalal Balkrishna Purani, *The Life of Sri Aurobindo (1872-1926)*, 2nd ed. (Pondicherry: Sri Aurobindo Ashram, 1960).

Haridas and Uma Mukherjee have constructed four studies that include detailed information on the political situation contemporary with Aurobindo's revolutionary involvement. See *"Bande Mataram" and Indian Nationalism (1906-08)* (Calcutta: Firma K. L. Mukhopadhyay, Presidency Library, 1957); *The Growth of Nationalism in India (1857-1905)*, 1st ed. (Calcutta: Presidency Library, 1957); *India's Fight for Freedom or The Swadeshi Movement (1905-06)*, 1st ed. (Calcutta: Firma K. L. Mukhopadhyay, 1958); *Sri Aurobindo and the New Thought in Indian Politics* (Calcutta: Firma K. L. Mukhopadhyay, 1964).

Also helpful on the partition of Bengal is P. C. Chakravarti, "Genesis of the Partition of Bengal (1905)," *The Modern Review* (April 1959), pp. 296-98.

Sisirkumar Mitra's *Resurgent India* (Bombay: Allied Publishers, 1963) is a valuable source for background on the resurgence in Indian life and the key figures who brought about the dramatic change, from Raja Rammohun Roy (1774-1833), the pioneer of modernism in Bengal, through to Sri Aurobindo Ghose, revolutionary, mystic, and poet.

2. According to Diwakar in *Mahayogi*, p. 33, it is not that Dr. Ghose disliked India but rather that he firmly believed that the good of India would come about chiefly through the impact and import of Western ways.

3. *On Himself*, 26: 1. Note that although Aurobindo's writings in this book take the shape of autobiographical reflections, he often speaks of himself in the third person since many of his remarks come as answers and corrections to his biographers.

4. *Ibid.*, p. 7.

5. During his Baroda days he married Mrinalini Devi (in 1901) with whom he lived infrequently. She died in 1918 en route to visit him in Pondicherry.

6. See *India's Fight for Freedom*, especially chap. 1. See also Keshavmurti, *Hope of Man*, p. 98, with a detailed footnote pertaining to this issue.

7. See *Imperial Gazetteer of India*, Bengal, vols. 1,2 for territorial configurations before and after partition; cited in Mukherjee and Mukherjee, *India's Fight for Freedom*, pp. 3-8 and p. 215, n5.

8. Mukherjee and Mukherjee, *India's Fight for Freedom*, pp. 8-12.

9. *Ibid.*, pp. 12-16. See also Karan Singh, *Prophet of Indian Nationalism: A*

Study of the Political Thought of Sri Aurobindo Ghosh 1893-1910 (London: George Allen & Unwin, 1963), pp. 106-7. In "Genesis of the Partition of Bengal (1905)," Chakravarti addresses the question of whether the partition was prompted by administrative conveniences or by political maneuverings. His study of correspondence among British leaders leads him to conclude that the partition was a subtle attack on the growing strength of Bengali nationalism.

10. *On Himself*, 26:29. See also Diwakar, *Mahayogi*, p. 63, Mukherjee and Mukherjee, *India's Fight for Freedom*, p. viii, Keshavmurti, *Hope of Man*, pp. 117-18, n 8.

11. Keshavmurti, *Hope of Man*, pp. 122-23; *On Himself*, 26: 46-48.

12. Keshavmurti, *Hope of Man*, p. 109.

13. *Bande Mataram and Indian Nationalism*, p. 18. In *Mahayogi*, p. 6, Diwakar writes that since 1885 the congress had functioned primarily as "an annual forum for ventilating political as well as other grievances against the government of the day."

14. *Bande Mataram and Indian Nationalism*, p. 20.

15. *On Himself*, 26:29-30.

16. *Ibid.*, p. 51.

17. N. K. Gupta, ed., *Sri Aurobindo and His Ashram*, 1st ed. (Calcutta: Arya Publishing House, 1948), p. 13. Mitra, *Resurgent India*, pp. 357-58.

18. *On Himself*, 26:22.

19. Diwakar, *Mahayogi*, p. 56; Karan Singh, *Prophet*, p. 104.

20. *On Himself*, 26:21.

21. Aurobindo himself approximates this date. *Ibid.*, p. 19.

22. *Ibid.*, pp. 50-51.

23. Diwakar, *Mahayogi*, pp. 72-75. For further details see Keshavmurti, *Hope of Man*, pp. 137-54.

24. *On Himself*, 26:33-34.

25. *Ibid.*, p. 34.

26. *Ibid.*, p. 35; cf. pp. 34-35.

27. *Ibid.*, p. 35. Aurobindo saw no British overture in this direction until 1919 with what were known as the Montagu Reforms. By then Aurobindo had retired from active political work. See Keshavmurti, *Hope of Man*, p. 226.

28. The name for Miss Margaret Noble, an Irish woman instrumental in the political life of India during this phase.

29. *On Himself*, 26:36.

30. *Ibid.*, pp. 36-37. For further details regarding these early days at Pondicherry see Keshavmurti, *Hope of Man*, pp. 197-209. Governmental records from this period together with excerpts from Indian and English newspapers have been collected and compiled in a very valuable book: Manoj Das, *Sri Aurobindo in the First Decade of the Century* (Pondicherry: Sri Aurobindo Ashram, 1972). The passages taken from the correspondence between Lord Minto (Viceroy) and Lord Morley (Secretary of State for India) regarding the likelihood of imprisoning

or deporting Aurobindo are particularly illuminating and illustrate the difficulty the English had in establishing a sound case against Aurobindo on the grounds of sedition. Aurobindo's sudden leave for Pondicherry was also interpreted by Minto as political in purpose: " . . . Arabindo is in Pondicherry where he seems to have formed some undesirable French connections and will probably sail for France . . ." (p. 138).

31. Quoted in Purani, *Life*, p. 120.

32. *On Himself*, 26: 37-39; see also p. 55.

33. *Ibid.*, p. 38.

34. *Ibid.*, p. 39. Keshavmurti, *Hope of Man*, pp. 307-14.

35. In an effort to engage India in fighting with the British against a common enemy, a member of the British cabinet, Stafford Cripps, proposed that if India joined Britain in the war, Britain would recognize her as an independent dominion with a new constitution and elected representatives at the end of the war. Keshavmurti, *Hope of Man*, pp. 315-16.

36. *On Himself*, 26:39.

37. *Ibid.*, p. 39.

38. *Ibid.*, p. 378.

39. The Mother is perceived as a divine embodiment of the transcendent and universal existence, bringing with her the supramental descent and allowing earth-consciousness to receive the supermind. Sri Aurobindo, *The Mother*, 25:47. Keshavmurti, *Hope of Man*, p. 211.

40. He "left his body" is a preferred expression among Indian sources. *Index*, 30: 5; Diwakar, *Mahayogi*, p. 98; and Mitra, *Liberator*, pp. 243-47.

2

Metaethical Perspective

Although the life and thought of Aurobindo reveal two strong urges, the political and the spiritual, the political inclinations are subordinate to and take their inspiration from his spiritual convictions.[1]

The revolution Aurobindo foresaw and fought for was a "spiritual revolution" where "the material [revolution] is only its shadow and reflex."[2] He saw from the start that his was a "moral and spiritual" task:[3]"It is the spirit alone that saves, and only by becoming great and free in heart can we become socially and politically great and free."[4] Aurobindo had illustrated this point in his speech "The Present Situation," addressed to a gathering at Bombay, January 19, 1908, where he developed his thought on nationalism not as a mere political program but as a religion from God in which nationalists function as God's instruments. Aurobindo details the demands of this role in a series of pointed questions that clearly indicate his position that the political program to liberate India was grounded in a spiritual conviction and commitment:

> If you are going to be a Nationalist, if you are going to assent to this religion of Nationalism, you must do it in the religious spirit. You must remember that you are the instruments of God . . . . Have you got a real faith? Or is it merely a political aspiration? Is it merely a larger kind of selfishness? Or is it merely that you wish to be free to oppress others, as you are being oppressed? Do you hold your political creed from a higher source? Is it God that is born in you? Have you realised that you are merely the instruments of God, that your bodies are not

31

your own? You are merely instruments of God for the work of the Almighty. Have you realised that? If you have realised that, then you are truly Nationalists; then alone will you be able to restore this great nation.[5]

The conviction about and the committment to that reality which Aurobindo here calls God ushers us into the one fundamental assumption undergirding Aurobindo's political and spiritual thought, namely, "that an Omnipresent Reality is at the basis of this universe."[6]

This omnipresent reality—also referred to as the Absolute, Sachchidananda, supreme reality, or Brahman—has three basic poises: the transcendent, the cosmic or universal, and the individual. The transcendent poise manifests itself in and through the cosmic and individual existence. It is in describing this process of manifestation that Aurobindo uncovers what becomes the central framework of his thought, "spiritual evolution."[7] This keynote of spiritual evolution is articulated in terms of a clearly outlined ontological structure and it is markedly teleological in impetus. The following discussion will center on these two reference points.

The Ontological Structure
of Spiritual Evolution

The ontological structure, or many levels of being, in Aurobindo's view of spiritual evolution is perhaps best visualized in the following schema:

Sachchidananda (Existence-Consciousness-Bliss; the Absolute)
Supermind (Dynamic Aspect of the Absolute)
Overmind (Mediating Plane between Individual Mind and Supermind)
Intuitive Mind
Illumined Mind
Higher Mind
Mind (Capable of intellectual knowledge, moving toward intuitional knowledge, through the higher levels approaching Supermind)
Soul or Psyche (Inner Self, True Self, Essential Self)
Life (Vital Level, Organic Level)
Matter or Body (The Inconscient)[8]

Sachchidananda contains *sat, chit*, and *ananda*, thus encompassing existence, consciousness-force, and bliss. This is Aurobindo's expression for the highest level of being and consciousness, the first and final referent of all existence. As consciousness-force it is designated as inherent in existence itself and immanent in all levels of being.[9] In human life it is present as consciousness, in animals and plants as the inconscient; it even abides in metals and, though not discernible to human beings, it is conscious to itself. In the supramental forms of being—that is, in forms higher than human consciousness—it exists in superconscience.[10] Bliss or delight refer to both the presence of this supreme reality and, as we shall see shortly, to the purpose of its self-manifestation: it is delight and manifests itself in order to share its delight. Bliss answers the *why* of evolution or creation.[11]

Supermind is the fullest spiritual consciousness and functions as the intermediary or the transition from the oneness of Sachchidananda to the multiplicity of the world; it alone contains the self-determining truth of the divine consciousness. Its very nature is indivisible knowledge. To be in the realm of supermind is to possess the divine omniscience and omnipotence; consequently the norms of the other levels of consciousness do not apply. To enter supramental awareness is to live consciously in the Supreme Sachchidananda.[12]

Overmind as a "delegate" of the supermind does not have the integral quality of the supramental truth nor the power to transform the entire natural order. Yet it is aware of the essential truth of things and does have the power to transform the individual and bring one into closer contact with supermind.[13] Intuition or intuitive mind knows directly through immediate inner contact rather than through the senses. Yet, unlike supermind, intuition sees things in moments or quick flashes rather than as a whole and reaches people through the heart as well as through the reason.[14] Illumined mind, not dependent on conceptual thought, works primarily by vision.[15] Higher mind on the other hand, closer to mind, is dominated by conceptual thought.[16]

Characteristic of the level of being in which human life participates, mind refers to that part of nature which deals "with cognition and intelligence, with ideas, with mental or thought perceptions" integrating reality through abstractions rather than through the concrete vision and the spiritual contact sought by the mystic.[17] Yet mind also participates in the higher levels of consciousness, the levels of higher mind, illumined mind, intuitive mind, and overmind, oriented as it is toward transcending itself in openness to supermind. As Bruteau points out, mind is not a being entirely different from supermind but rather participates in supermind in a limited, diminished, unclear way.[18]

The soul or psyche (conscious form of the soul) is the immortal principle of the divine within the individual, enabling the evolution from ignorance to light.[19]

Life is cosmic energy, which initially expresses itself in human life in desiring and destroying the persons and possessions of others. In later stages desire is manifested in mutuality and love, where life becomes indispensable for spiritual realization. Through life the divine existence is manifest and is received.[20]

Matter, as the stuff of physical existence, is also form and habitation of spirit and the locus for spirit-realization.[21] Matter is not reducible to mere material substance because it is a form that the universal spirit has assumed in its descent from Sachchidananda, giving energy and life.[22] The world itself is seen as the manifestation of the divine existence, consciousness-force, and bliss. As a manifestation of the Real it is itself real.[23]

Thus Aurobindo sees Sachchidananda as ineffable in nature, both permeating and transcending the cosmic existence, which is itself a determination of the pure being. In his view however, this pure being manifests itself continuously in an evolutionary process with clear teleological directions. To understand Aurobindo's metaphysics we must see it not only in hierarchical imagery but in spiral and cyclic imagery suggesting motion.[24] The spiritual evolution is happening.

The Teleological Impetus
of Spiritual Evolution

In Aurobindo's view of spiritual evolution, exclusive emphasis is placed neither on being nor on becoming. The whole of reality is perceived in a process perspective in which the supreme reality is ever being and becoming manifest in the many levels of being. Evolution is the method by which consciousness liberates itself.[25] This is due not to caprice, nor to chance, but to an inner law of necessity directing the evolutionary course.[26] And yet the teleological thrust does not suggest incompleteness on the part of Sachchidananda, which is the fulness of existence, consciousness, and bliss. Rather, the purposive orientation of evolution has to do with the world. Spiritual evolution then becomes

> a series of ascents from the physical being and consciousness to the vital, the being dominated by the life-self, thence to the mental being realised in the fully developed man and thence into the perfect consciousness which is beyond the mental, into the Supramental consciousness and the Supramental being, the Truth-Consciousness which is the integral consciousness of the spiritual being. Mind cannot be our last conscious expression because mind is fundamentally an ignorance seeking for knowledge; it is only the Supramental Truth-Consciousness that can bring us the true and the whole Self-Knowledge and world-knowledge; it is through that only that we can get to our true being and fulfilment of our spiritual evolution.[27]

The impetus in Aurobindo's spiritual evolution is two-fold: a pressure from above and an impulse from below, which together enable a gradual unfoldment of the supreme existence.[28] The pressure from above calls the lower forms to evolve out of their limitedness and break through to a new stage of consciousness. The primordial starting point of evolution is named "involution": the entry of the spirit into the inconscient. The order of involution[29] is that of existence through consciousness-force, bliss, supermind, through to the level of matter. It is this involution of the spirit that makes evolution possible. The one implies the other. Evolution presumes involution; involution then expresses itself in a reverse movement, evolution.

Evolution as the other term of the process, then, refers to the self-unfolding of the supreme spirit from the realm of inconscient matter through the mental and supramental levels to Sachchidananda as supreme existence. In a word, evolution is possible because spirit is presently involved in inconscient matter; evolution is purposive in that it is the gradual manifestation of the spirit's presence in all levels of being for the sheer delight of sharing itself. Chaudhuri refers to this as "a kind of purposeless purpose . . . the purpose of creative joy, of Being's joyful self-expression."[30]

Since human beings alone, unlike lower levels of life and inconscience, are able to participate in evolution reflectively, it is their task to consciously help nature in their own physical and spiritual evolution in order to effect the triple transformation.[31] The three-fold dimension of this transformation is crucial. Aurobindo insists that the transformation must include: a psychic change in which the whole person is converted into a "soul-instrumentation"; a spiritual change in which even the lowest dimensions of life, body, and subconscience, are permeated by the descent and presence of a "higher Light, Knowledge, Power, Force, Bliss, Purity"; and third, the "supramental transmutation," that is, "the ascent into the Supermind and the transforming descent of the supramental Consciousness into our entire being and nature."[32]

Given this teleological orientation it becomes clear that Aurobindo's image of history is linear in contrast to India's traditional cyclical image of history as an endless revolution of the four ages. History is perceived as going somewhere. A new order of being and knowing is now possible to those who radically open themselves to the divine.[33]

Fundamental to Aurobindo's entire perspective is his conviction that there is in human beings an eternal urge to grow.[34] He encourages this urge to grow by emphasizing the beauty and value of yoga, that discipline by which one helps to bring about the triple transformation that is the goal of evolution. The evolutionary goal of the world and the individual's power to help it happen point to the intimate connection between evolution and yoga.[35]

Like evolution, yoga must respect and integrate matter, life, and mind in its thrust to break through to the supramental consciousness and to realize Sachchidananda. Again, like evolution, Aurobindo's integral yoga aims not at denial or rejection but at the transformation of all levels of being. Finally, like evolution, yoga is not only individual but cosmic in its orientation and expectation. However, whereas evolution proceeds slowly and indirectly, seeking the divine through nature, yoga functions more quickly and directly, reaching out for the divine as transcendent to nature.[36]

Yoga for Aurobindo is the growth from normal and therefore limited human consciousness into higher and expanded divine consciousness. It is, in essence, "the union of the soul with the immortal being and consciousness and delight of the Divine"[37] in such a way that the divine consciousness and the peace, light, joy, and knowledge it brings are integrated into human nature.

The goal of all traditional yogas has been *mukti* or liberation. Since the world is perceived within these traditional perspectives as transient or illusory, the goal of the awakened individual would be release from the cycle of birth and death. However, because for Aurobindo the world is the willed emanation of the divine,[38] it is not to be escaped from but is to be transformed according to Integral Yoga. And because the individual is also a partial manifestation of the divine, the human body is not to be silenced nor rejected, but is to be accepted and disciplined in a way that will enable it to become pure, supple, and responsive to the divine consciousness present within it. In a word, the Integral Yoga of Aurobindo is designed not to encourage escape from life but rather to encourage an embrace of life in a growth leading to full participation in the life divine.[39]

Though lengthy, the following excerpt from Aurobindo is presented here to convey the full flavor of his own assessment of Integral Yoga.

I have never said that my Yoga was something brand new in all its elements. I have called it the integral Yoga and that means that it takes up the essence and many processes of the old Yogas—its newness is in its aim, standpoint and the totality of its method . . . . I do not . . . care in the least . . . whether this Yoga and its aim and method are accepted as new or not; that is in itself a trifling matter. That it should be recognised as true in itself by those who can accept or practise it and should make itself true by achievement is the one thing important; it does not matter if it is called new or a repetition or revival of the old which was forgotten. I laid emphasis on it as new in a letter to certain sadhaks so as to explain to them that a repetition of the aim and idea of the old Yogas was not enough in my eyes, that I was putting forward a thing to be achieved that has not yet been achieved, not yet clearly visualised, even though it is one natural but still secret outcome of all the past spiritual endeavour.

It is new as compared with the old Yogas:

(1) Because it aims not at a departure out of world and life into Heaven or Nirvana, but a change of life and existence, not as something subordinate or incidental, but as a distinct and central object. If there is a descent in other Yogas, yet it is only an incident on the way or resulting from the ascent—the ascent is the real thing. Here the ascent is the first step, but it is a means for the descent. It is the descent of the

new consciousness attained by the ascent that is the stamp and seal of the sadhana. Even the Tantra and Vaishnavism end in the release from life; here the object is the divine fulfilment of life.

(2) Because the object sought after is not an individual achievement of divine realisation for the sake of the individual, but something to be gained for the earth-consciousness here, a cosmic, not solely a supra-cosmic achievement. The thing to be gained also is the bringing in of a Power of Consciousness (the Supramental) not yet organised or active directly in earth-nature, even in the spiritual life, but yet to be or-ganised and made directly active.

(3) Because a method has been preconized for achieving this pur-pose which is as total and integral as the aim set before it, viz., the total and integral change of the consciousness and nature, taking up old methods but only as a part action and present aid to others that are distinctive. I have not found this method (as a whole) or anything like it professed or realised in the old Yogas. If I had, I should not have wasted my time in hewing out paths and in thirty years of search and inner creation when I could have hastened home safely to my goal in an easy canter over paths already blazed out, laid down, perfectly mapped, macadamised, made secure and public. Our Yoga is not a retreading of old walks, but a spiritual adventure.[40]

The presupposition on which this yoga depends is "an inner call for the Divine" experienced by the individual who then surrenders the self totally—"soul, mind, heart, sense, will, life, body."[41] The value of this surrender is pivotal for the yogi and consists basically in a growing trust and confidence in the divine:

> Self-giving or surrender is demanded because without such a progres-sive surrender of the being it is quite impossible to get anywhere near the goal. To keep open means to call in the Force to work in you, and if you do not surrender to it, it amounts to not allowing the Force to work in you at all or else only on condition that it will work in the way you want and not in its own way which is the way of the Divine Truth.[42]

Surrender to the divine brings about the transformation of the indi-vidual through the transition from mind to supermind. One's own delib-erate discipline and effort play a critical role in the transformation that is sought. And yet, while the individual's surrender and yogic practice are crucial in the evolution, Aurobindo continually maintains that due to the transcendent poise of the divine, ultimately "it rests with the Divine will to choose the time and occasion for the Divine Descent, without which this realisation is impossible.''[43]

Through yoga individual practitioners assume greater control over both body and mind, and open themselves to supermind and the liberation that comes through the triple transformation. Yet, this yoga does not annihilate, reject, or escape from the body for it is based upon the transformation of the lower by the higher, and the consequent ascent of the lower with the higher in a new (transformed) way of being.[44]

> By transformation I do not mean some change of the nature—I do not mean, for instance, sainthood or ethical perfection or Yogic Siddhis (like the Tantrik's) or a transcendental (*cinmaya*) body. I use transformation in a special sense, a change of consciousness radical and complete and of a certain specific kind which is so conceived as to bring about a strong and assured step forward in the spiritual evolution of the being of a greater and higher kind and of a larger sweep and completeness than what took place when a mentalised being first appeared in a vital and material animal world. If anything short of that takes place or at least if a real beginning is not made on that basis, a fundamental progress toward this fulfilment, then my object is not accomplished. A partial realisation, something mixed and inconclusive, does not meet the demand I make on life and Yoga.[45]

The transformed individual is the gnostic being—the superman, who enjoys ''fuller life-power,'' ''fuller body-power''[46]—that being whose entire being is governed by universal spirit, recognizing the divine everywhere in the world. At this stage, each person will be bound not by an individual law but by the divine law, which is a law of unity, mutuality, and harmony. At the gnostic stage of existence the ethical dimension is transcended, since all actions proceed directly from divine knowledge and divine self-determination..

For Aurobindo, ethics refers to a set of laws and guides that give direction to people who experience conflict and tension between their own self-centered concerns and their realization of spiritual ideals. Once the movement toward gnostic transformation is complete, the ethical norms and guides are no longer necessary because conflict and tension are no longer experienced. Ethics is a means in the struggle of spiritual seeking. When the goal is achieved, the means becomes unnecessary and dysfunctional. A new law emerges: the divine law of harmony and universality rooted in conscient oneness with all beings.

> The ethical impulse and attitude, so all-important to humanity, is a means by which it struggles out of the lower harmony and universality based upon inconscience and broken up by Life into individual discords towards a higher harmony and universality based upon conscient oneness with all existences. Arriving at that goal, this means will no longer be necessary or even possible, since the qualities and oppositions on which it depends will naturally dissolve and disappear in the final reconciliation.[47]

Evolution is the urge of Sachchidananda toward self-expression; at first it is nonethical or at least infraethical, until it expresses itself in human life, which is the context for the ethical realm. As the urge proceeds to supramental expression, it becomes supraethical. At the gnostic level there is neither ignorance nor evil.[48]

Summary

The discussion has revealed that inquiry into the metaethical perspective of Aurobindo demands a recognition of the conscious connections between the political and the spiritual dimensions of life, and a consideration of his concept of spiritual evolution.

Within this horizon, it becomes clear that for Aurobindo Ghose the Divine, Brahman, Supreme Reality, or Spirit are names for Sachchidananda, that is, existence, consciousness-force, and bliss, which is understood to have involved itself in the various levels of being through a movement of descent. This involution or descending movement accounts for the cosmic and universal poise of Sachchidananda, which is seen to pervade supermind, mind, soul, life, and matter. The evolution or ascending motion whereby the subconscient and conscient levels of being are constantly moving toward supraconscient being reveals the individual poise of Sachchidananda and also gives clarity to the life-context in which people find themselves.

In this vision, space and time become cosmic forms of the spirit's self-manifestation and self-expression: the world reveals the spirit, and time is conceived in historical, linear, and spiral imagery as that matrix through which all things are called to progress toward transformation.

Since human beings are the human frame embodying Sachchidananda inadequately and imperfectly, they are called to surrender themselves in radical openness to the divine and to help bring about the evolutionary progress through disciplined practice of integral yoga. Through the complementarity of evolution and yoga, the ultimate good of human life (transformation into the life divine) will be achieved in a trans-ethical gnostic stage of existence, the goal and destiny of the evolutionary thrust.

It is now timely to question Aurobindo with respect to the sources of his thought. Do his positions, for example, ultimately derive from his educational influences, his yogic experiences, or from the Hindu scriptures?

Sources of Thought

Certainly Aurobindo is indebted to the influences of his early educational years in England, and to his political and yogic experiences, as well as to the literary and scriptural heritage of Hinduism. His educational influences encompass not only the formalized studies scheduled for him in England but also the years in India when he immersed himself in the riches of his tradition—its literature, language, and culture. *The Foundations of Indian Culture* makes it clear that Aurobindo sees himself as part of the tradition of the Vedas and Vedanta; *The Life Divine* is written within a consciousness of and as a reaffirmation of the Upanishads; the Gita prompted Aurobindo to write numerous essays and to develop his own style of karmayoga.[49] His thought is punctuated with references to the Vaishnava concept of divine lila (play) as well as the Tantric notion of Kali (Mother). Although he does not often cite names, he was undoubtedly familiar with Bergson's concept of creative evolution and Nietzsche's notion of the superman.[50]

Because his understanding of reality is one that transcends conceptual knowledge, Aurobindo claims that the true realization of reality implies a supraconceptual consciousness, a transrational awareness rooted in *experience*, which brings with it the highest form of knowledge one can attain.[51] Maitra has observed: "If there is one formula by which the whole of his philosophy can be summed up ... it is the imperative necessity of rising above the intellect."[52] Aurobindo describes it as a process of discovering "the deeper Truth behind."[53]

In his 1908 speech entitled "The Present Situation," Aurobindo sharply criticizes the role of intellectual knowledge in a defense of the nationalists whose opponents are men of esteemed and recognized intellectual ability, yet whose very intellects narrow their horizon and lead them to despair.

> The only conclusion is that there is nothing to be done. The only conclusion is that this country is doomed. That is the conclusion to which this intellectual process will lead you.[54]

What is his alternative? A fuller source for knowledge is *belief*, which "is not a merely intellectual process ... not a mere persuasion of the mind," but "something that is in our heart, and what you believe, you must do, because belief is from God. It is to the heart that God speaks, it is in the heart that God resides."[55]

Bengal heard the "voice of God"[56] and it was this faith that enabled Bengal to gain strength in awakening the nationalist spirit within.

> Often they do not understand what they are doing. They do not always realise who guides or where he will guide them; but they have this conviction within, not in the intellect but in the heart, that the Power that is guiding them is invincible, that it is almighty, that it is immortal and irresistible and that it will do its work. They have nothing to do. They have simply to obey that Power ... to go where it leads them ... to speak the words that it tells them to speak, and to do the thing that it tells them to do .... God is doing everything. We are not doing anything.[57]

This for Aurobindo is faith, selflessness, courage—a religion, not a mere political program of self-interest[58]—"the doing of that Truth within you ... that immortal Power within you" who called upon Bengal to do his work.[59]

The experience of God within is clearly a decisive source of knowledge for Aurobindo during the days of his intense nationalist activities as well as his days as a yogi at Pondicherry.[60] For example, this "voice of God within" came to him clearly while he was in the Alipore jail, and in this experience he came to a new understanding of himself and a new perception that he was speaking not on his own authority but on the authority of Lord Krishna.

> This is the word that has been put into my mouth to speak to you today. What I intended to speak has been put away from me, and beyond what is given to me I have nothing to say. It is only the word that is put into me that I can speak to you. That word is now finished. I spoke once before with this force in me and I said then that this movement is not a political movement and that nationalism is not politics but a religion, a creed, a faith. I say it again today, but I put it in another way. I say no longer that nationalism is a creed, a religion, a faith; I say that it is the Sanatan Dharma [eternal religion] which for us is nationalism. This Hindu nation was born with the Sanatan Dharma, with it it moves and with it it grows. When the Sanatan Dharma declines, then the nation declines, and if the Sanatan Dharma were capable of perishing, with the Sanatan Dharma it would perish. The Sanatan Dharma, that is nationalism. This is the message that I have to speak to you.[61]

Aurobindo's distrust of reason to make judgments about what pertains to the suprarational realm of consciousness is evident also in his writings on yoga. He considered yoga to be a more adequate source for suprarational knowledge. Even in spite of one-time agnostic inclinations, Aurobindo consistently affirmed supra-physical reality and consciousness.

> I have had too my period of agnostic denial, but from the moment I looked at these things I could never take the attitude of doubt and disbelief which was for so long fashionable in Europe. Abnormal, otherwise supra-physical experiences and powers, occult or Yogic, have always seemed to me something perfectly natural and credible. Consciousness in its very nature could not be limited by the ordinary physical human-animal consciousness, it must have the other ranges. Yogic or occult powers are no more supernatural or incredible than is supernatural or incredible the power to write a great poem or compose great music; few people can do it, as things are,—not even one in a million; for poetry and music come from the inner being and to write or to compose true and great things one has to have the passage clear between the outer mind and something in the inner being . . . . Of course, the first thing is to believe, aspire and, with the true urge within, make the endeavour.[62]

Consequently, reason and its popular expression in science are for Aurobindo inadequate, incomplete, and therefore ultimately untrustworthy.[63]

The understandings released through yoga have a law of their own not shared by science or the ordinary reason. Rather, the yogi must develop an "intuitive discrimination" that analyzes the experiences in terms of suggested methods of the guru and systems of the past and also within their context of spiritual phenomena.[64] The yogi must seek answers not from "the logical intellect trying to co-ordinate its ignorance," but "from higher spiritual experience, from a deeper source of knowledge."[65]

Ultimately, however, the yogi must develop an intuitive power, which becomes in the final analysis the most trustworthy faculty for discernment. Since there are many levels and types of intuition for Aurobindo, the source of the intuition determines its value. If it originates in or is controlled by the mind, it is deficient and this deficiency and its attendant ignorance will dissolve only when the supermind descends into the mind and touches the psychic being within. Genuine intuitional experiences come both from above and from within—from the supermind and also from the psychic representative of the Divine.

In his own search for union with the Absolute, Aurobindo became less and less dependent on sources outside of himself, even Ramakrishna and Vivekananda, who were for a time significant sources in his spiritual seeking.[66]

> As the Yoga increased, I read very little—for when all the ideas in the world come crowding from within or from above, there is not much need for gathering mental food from outside sources; at most a utility for keeping oneself informed of what is happening in the world,—but not as material for building up one's vision of the world and Truth and things. One becomes an independent mind in communion with the cosmic Thinker.[67]

This communion enables the individual to rise above the intellect and to enter the illumined consciousness of the supermind, which is the end and aim of the integral yoga and also the source of truth.[68]

Supramental consciousness, the goal of integral yoga, is marked by an intense awareness of union with the Spiritual Reality. Langley likens it to aesthetic experience in that the consciousness of spirit is a kind of "kinship": "simple, direct, intimate and personal."[69] Or it is like the knowledge that arises through personal relationships, with the central analogue being a knowledge that arises from union, in contrast to scientific knowledge, which arises from observing, scrutinizing, and analyzing the object to be known as apart and separate from the knower.[70]

Review

In looking at the sources of Aurobindo's thought it becomes clear that the categories of the question posed in the preface (are the sources theonomous? autonomous?) are not fully adequate to deal with the content of the response. On the one hand we might say that Aurobindo's sources of thought are rooted neither in a heteronomous source such as divine revelation nor in an autonomous source such as personal insight or intuition. On the other hand we might say that they are rooted in both. The very terms of the question suggest polarity and it is precisely this duality of the divine and the human, the (supreme) spirit and the (individual) self that Aurobindo attempts to dissolve in the metaphysics he constructs. And such a metaphysics profoundly influences his epistemology. For to Aurobindo, only to the extent that one is truly open to the divine does one share in the consciousness of the divine.

Ultimately the most significant source of knowledge within this system is experience of the divine. But the divine is not imaged as an out-there phenomenon distant spatially, temporally, or psychologically. Rather, the divine is a radically "in-here," in-the-heart phenomenon, identical with the individual who surrenders, willing to experience and express divine transcendence in individual and cosmic existence.

As the whole of chapter 2 has demonstrated, Aurobindo claims to have constructed a metaphysics that reconciles spirit and matter by grounding both in the reality of a transcendental and cosmic consciousness. He claims simply to be articulating the truth of his experience, which brings a knowledge from beyond and therefore is not subject to rational, scientific investigation. But he is not appealing to an act of faith either. He claims that the experience he enjoys is open to anyone willing to surrender to the divine and determined to practice integral yoga. It is this surrender and this effort, together with the divine descent, that release such understandings.

At this point, having sketched the background of Aurobindo's life and the metaphysical perspective undergirding his thought, I am ready to address the main interest of the inquiry: freedom, or liberation. This interest is prompted by Aurobindo's personal and political commitment to work for India's liberation, and his personal, spiritual commitment to work for the liberation of humanity. The questions posed to Aurobindo's thought, as outlined in the preface, touch several bases: what is political freedom and what is spiritual freedom at each period of his life? are political freedom and spiritual freedom means to some other ends, or are they ends in themselves? how are political freedom and spiritual freedom related, in the political (pre-1910) period and in the spiritual (post-1910) period?

Notes

1. Diwakar, *Mahayogi*, p. 64; see also *On Himself*, 26: 98-99.

2. "The Ideal of the Karmayogin" (June 19, 1909), in *Karmayogin*, 2: 17.

3. *Ibid.*, p. 16.

4. *Ibid.*, p. 18.

5. *Bande Mataram*, 1: 652-53; also "Uttarpara Speech" (1909), in *Karmayogin*, 2: 9-10.

6. Ambalal Balkrishna Purani, *Sri Aurobindo's Life Divine: Lectures Delivered in the USA*, 1st ed. (Pondicherry: Sri Aurobindo Ashram, 1966), pp. 269-70. In *On Himself*, 26: 95, Aurobindo writes: "The teaching of Sri Aurobindo starts from that of the ancient sages of India that behind the appearances of the universe there is the Reality of a Being and Consciousness, a Self of all things, one and eternal. All beings are united in that One Self and Spirit but divided by a certain separativity of consciousness, an ignorance of their true Self and Reality in the mind, life and body. It is possible by a certain psychological discipline to remove this veil of separative consciousness and become aware of the true Self, the Divinity within us and all." See also *Letters on Yoga*, 22: 236. A central secondary source on the many dimensions of consciousness in Aurobindo's thought is Satprem, *Sri Aurobindo or the Adventure of Consciousness*, trans. Tehmi (Pondicherry: Sri Aurobindo Ashram, 1970).

After he had retired to Pondicherry, Aurobindo wrote in a letter to Joseph Baptista (1920): "I do not at all look down on politics or political action or consider I have got above them. I have always laid a dominant stress and I now lay an entire stress on the spiritual life, but my idea of spirituality has nothing to do with ascetic withdrawal or contempt or disgust of secular things. There is to me nothing secular, all human activity is for me a thing to be included in a complete spiritual life . . ." (*On Himself*, 26: 430).

7. *Life Divine*, 19: 824. Aurobindo does not argue the pros and cons of evolutionary theory but takes it as an established scientific fact. He then discusses

evolution in terms of spiritual reality as well as sense data. See also *The Problem of Rebirth*, 16: 97-98, Bruteau, *World*, p. 261, and Reddy, *Evolution*, especially pp. 49ff. for an interesting survey and discussion on evolution.

8. See also Robert A. McDermott, "Sri Aurobindo: An Integrated Theory of Individual and Historical Transformation," *International Philosophical Quarterly* 12, no. 2 (June 1972): 175; in *World*, pp. 123-27, Bruteau offers additional diagrams. Other sources helpful in acquainting the student with Aurobindo's concept of spiritual evolution include: *The Integral Philosophy of Sri Aurobindo: A Commemorative Symposium*, ed. Haridas Chaudhuri and Frederic Spiegelberg (London: George Allen & Unwin, 1960); Laxman Ganpatrao Chincholkar, *A Critical Study of Aurobindo: with Special Reference to his Concept of Spiritual Evolution* (Nagpur, 1966?); McDermott, "THE LIFE DIVINE: Sri Aurobindo's Philosophy of Evolution and Transformation," in *Six Pillars: Introductions to the Major Works of Sri Aurobindo*, ed. R. A. McDermott (New York: Schocken, 1974), pp. 161-91; Reddy, *Evolution*; Ram Nath Sharma, *The Philosophy of Sri Aurobindo*, 2nd ed. (Meerut: Kedar Nath Ram Nath, 1963); Nathaniel Pearson, *Sri Aurobindo and the Soul-Quest of Man: Three Steps to Spiritual Knowledge* (London: George Allen & Unwin, 1952); Purani, *Life Divine*; Herbert Jai Singh, *Sri Aurobindo: His Life and Religious Thought* (Bangalore: Christian Institute for the Study of Religion and Society, 1962).

9. The close connection between consciousness and existence is notably characteristic of integral philosophy, according to Haridas Chaudhuri, *The Philosophy of Integralism: The Metaphysical Synthesis in Sri Aurobindo's Teaching*, 2nd enl. ed. (Pondicherry: Sri Aurobindo Ashram, 1967), p. 38. See also Reddy, *Evolution*, p. 148, and S. K. Maitra, *The Meeting of the East and the West in Sri Aurobindo's Philosophy* (Pondicherry: Sri Aurobindo Ashram, 1968), pp. 6-9, where the author indicates this triple designation of reality to be the traditional contribution of Indian philosophy.

This notion of consciousness-force or conscious energy central to Aurobindo's entire system derives from the traditional Indian concept of *Sakti* or divine creative energy, as well as from the concept of *chit* or divine consciousness. Bruteau writes, "Shakti is energy, power, strength, force, activity; it is related to the concrete, the manifest, the dynamic, and is distinguished from *Siva*, the principle of transcendence" (*World*, pp. 48-49). In a footnote on p. 49, Bruteau explains: "In India the Shakti principle is regarded as feminine and is worshipped as the Divine Mother under various aspects. The tantric tradition especially has developed this cult, and there are strong resemblances between its tenets and those of Aurobindo." See also Chaudhuri, *Integralism*, p. 71.

10. H. J. Singh, *Sri Aurobindo*, pp. 10-12; Chaudhuri, *Integralism*, p. 39.

11. H. J. Singh, *Sri Aurobindo*, p. 13; Reddy, *Evolution*, pp. 185-86. According to Maitra in *Meeting of East and West*, p. 34, evolution is the inverse of the process of creation and creation the inverse of evolution. This will become evident in the discussion on involution and evolution, and ascent and descent.

12. *Letters on Yoga*, 22: 240-41; *Dictionary of Sri Aurobindo's Yoga*, comp. M. P. Pandit (Pondicherry: Dipti Publications, Sri Aurobindo Ashram, 1966), pp. 252-53. Also *Synthesis of Yoga*, 21: 599.

13. *Dictionary*, pp. 177-78. Also McDermott, "An Integrated Theory," p. 177.

14. *Dictionary*, p. 134.

15. *Life Divine*, 19: 944-45.

16. *Ibid.*, p. 941.

17. *Dictionary*, p. 158; H. J. Singh, *Sri Aurobindo*, pp. 14-15.

18. *World*, p. 94. Yet, since it is capable of ignorance, it is also a power of ignorance. *Synthesis of Yoga*, 21: 599.

19. *Dictionary*, pp. 239-40.

20. H. J. Singh, *Sri Aurobindo*, p. 18; *Dictionary*, pp. 145-46.

21. *Life Divine*, 18: 6; *Dictionary*, p. 155.

22. H. J. Singh, *Sri Aurobindo*, p. 18; *Synthesis of Yoga*, 21: 600.

23. *On Himself*, 26: 105; Sharma, *Philosophy*, p. 114. On this issue of the reality of the world, Aurobindo is definite in disclaiming any agreement with Sankara that cosmic existence is an illusion, an unreality, maya, though he is tolerant toward others who may find this interpretation satisfying. See *On Himself*, 26: 102-6. On the contrary, Aurobindo holds that cosmic existence is a manifestation and determination of the pure being. The energy that sustains the cosmic manifestations is an energy of the being and both the being and its determinations are real. See *Life Divine*, 18: 25-32, also the discussion on pp. 439-81. And so he refers to his philosophy as Purnadvaita, integral nondualism in contrast to two prominent Indian positions: Sankara's Kevaladvaita, unqualified nondualism on the one hand, and Ramanuja's Vishishtadvaita, on the other hand, the position of qualified nondualism (in which the world is real but, insofar as it is the body of God, is totally dependent). Aurobindo's "Purna" is designed to carry a stronger intrinsic value of the world without at the same time suggesting any separation from God. See Bruteau, *World*, pp. 41-42; especially chap. 5, pp. 152-90, for a detailed and lucid discussion of Aurobindo's position regarding the maya position of Sankara. Also Chaudhuri, *Integralism*, pp. 1-3, 31-34; Reddy, *Evolution*, pp. 187-97. The philosophical positions of Sankara and Ramanuja are delineated in Surendranath Dasgupta, *A History of Indian Philosophy*, 5 vols. (Cambridge: University Press, 1922-55), especially vols. 1, 2, 3.

24. "Yoga and Human Evolution," in *Harmony of Virtue*, 3: 357-58; *Life Divine*, 19: 1046; "Evolution," in *Supramental Manifestation*, 16: 229.

25. *On Himself*, 26: 95.

26. H. J. Singh, *Sri Aurobindo*, p. 9; Bruteau, *World*, p. 230, n28. Discussion of the question of determinism will be resumed in chapters 3 and 4 of this study.

27. *Dictionary*, p. 244.

28. Chincholkar, *Critical Study*, p. 81. See G. H. Langley, *Sri Aurobindo: Indian Poet, Philosopher and Mystic* (London: D. Marlowe for the Royal India and Pakistan Society, 1949), pp. 69-81 for a brief but insightful discussion on the ascent-descent dialectic in Aurobindo's theory. Bruteau, *World*, pp. 36-37; Reddy, *Evolution*, pp. 229-36, 255-56.

29. What Maitra calls "creation": "the movement downward from the Spirit." *Meeting of East and West*, p. 47.

30. *Integralism*, p. 100. "It is not procuring something from without, but objectifying something from within. It is actualizing the riches of inwardness. It is the spontaneous overflow of inward fulness" (*ibid*.). Chaudhuri then relates his point in a delightful image: "After a day's hard labor and weariness, when a person takes a hearty meal and relaxes on the sofa, he begins to feel again very full inside. What does he want to do then? Out of a sense of inward fulness, he may feel like singing or dancing, or writing poetry or playing a game. Such activities are neither meaningless nor utilitarian. They are a joyful outpouring of the inner self. Similarly, evolution is a spontaneous unfoldment of the creative urge of Being" (*ibid*.).

It is on the basis of this teleological interpretation of evolution that Aurobindo differs from the Sankhya position. Aurobindo holds that the Sankhya position on unconscious teleology is untenable and claims that there is an intelligent, creative (purposive) force behind and within the evolutionary process. Whereas the Sankhya philosophy claims that of the two principles of life, Prakriti and Purusha, Prakriti (Nature) is unconscious and all consciousness is then ascribed to the principle of Purusha, which is present to but detached from Prakriti, Aurobindo's position is that all levels of being are permeated with consciousness, even though in the lower levels it appears as inconscient. See Bruteau, *World*, p. 58; Chaudhuri, *Integralism*, p. 106; Reddy, *Evolution*, p. 248n; *On Himself*, 26: 105.

31. Part of the uniqueness in human life is also evident in a double involvement in being by virtue of human participation in subconscience and superconscience. Reddy, *Evolution*, p. 268.

32. *Life Divine*, 19: 891; *On Himself*, 26: 118. Because in Aurobindo's theory of evolution the psychic being is affected as well as other levels of life, Maitra points to the uniqueness of this concept of evolution that includes the *inward* movement as well as the upward and downward movement. See *Meeting of East and West*, p. 99. See also Madhav Pundalik Pandit's description of the superman in *Sadhana in Sri Aurobindo's Yoga* (Pondicherry (?), 1962), pp. 18-22.

33. Bruteau, *World*, pp. 230-31; *On Himself*, 26: 125; on not limiting the present by the past, p. 134.

34. "Yoga and Human Evolution," *Harmony of Virtue*, 3: 358; "Our Ideals," *Supramental Manifestation*, 16: 308. Bruteau paraphrases Aurobindo's conviction: "the very core of man . . . is the necessity to exceed himself." *World*, p. 131. See also Chaudhuri, *Integralism*, pp. 131-32 on the "self-transcending urge."

35. Bruteau, *World*, pp. 129-30; Maitra, *Meeting of East and West*, pp. 157-58.

36. Sharma, *Philosophy*, pp. 170-71. See *Synthesis of Yoga*, 20: 2, where Aurobindo writes that "all life . . . is a vast Yoga of Nature . . .".

37. *Dictionary*, p. 310.

38. Bruteau highlights the fact that Aurobindo uses both emanationist and creationist language when speaking of the relationship between Brahman and the world. His language is emanationist insofar as Brahman is seen in cosmic and individual poises, yet creationist insofar as Brahman is seen as transcendent source of the involutionary-evolutionary movement. *World*, pp. 47-49, 256.

39. *On Himself*, 26: 99; Maitra, *Meeting of East and West*, pp. 155-63; Pandit, *Sadhana*, pp. 27-31; Purani, *Life Divine*, p. 3.

40. *On Himself*, 26: 107-9, dated 5/10/35.

41. Sharma, *Philosophy*, pp. 172-73. On the psychic dimension as the most important, see Reddy, *Evolution*, p. 290.

42. *Dictionary*, p. 263.

43. Reddy, *Evolution*, pp. 149-50.

44. Sharma, *Philosophy*, p. 169; see *On Himself*, 26: 117-18.

45. *On Himself*, 26: 106-7.

46. *Ibid.*, p. 124.

47. *Life Divine*, 18: 97.

48. *Ibid.*, pp. 97-99; for further references in Aurobindo on the problem of evil, see "The Principle of Evil," in *Harmony of Virtue*, 3: 383-86 and "The Origin and Remedy of Falsehood, Error, Wrong and Evil," in *Life Divine*, 18: 596-632. See also, Reddy, *Evolution*, pp. 324-26nn; Sharma, *Philosophy*, pp. 176, 144; Chincholkar, *Critical Study*, pp. 176-78; Chaudhuri, *Integralism*, pp. 180-81; for an extended discussion, see Maitra, *Meeting of East and West*, chapter 3, "Sri Aurobindo and the Problem of Evil," pp. 111-50.
Bruteau criticizes Aurobindo on this issue, naming the problem of evil to be "the most questionable element" in his system (*World*, pp. 270-71). In *The Political Philosophy of Sri Aurobindo* (New York: Asia Publishing House, 1960), p. 134, V. P. Varma refers to the "almost Hegelian rationalization and justification of evil, war, hatred and sorrow as forces in history."

49. *On Himself*, 26: 126-29.

50. *The Supramental Manifestation*, 16: 275; *Hour of God*, 17: 388-90; *Letters on Yoga*, 22: 213; Varma, *Political Philosophy*, p. 134; H. J. Singh, *Sri Aurobindo*, pp. 7-8; Maitra, *Meeting of East and West*, pp. 66-110 for an essay on Aurobindo and Bergson. On tantrism and Sri Aurobindo, see Kees W. Bolle, *The Persistence of Religion: An Essay on Tantrism and Sri Aurobindo's Philosophy*, with a preface by Mircea Eliade (London: E. J. Brill, 1965).

51. Bruteau offers a summary of four key experiences or yogic realizations on which the intellectual exposition of Aurobindo's philosophy is based. These are: 1) his yogic experience of nirvana during his involvement in the independence movement; 2) the vision of Sri Krishna at the Alipore jail; 3) the time at Chandernagore in 1910 while en route to Pondicherry; and 4) November 24, 1926, the day of *siddhi* at Pondicherry (*World*, pp. 23-40).

52. *Studies in Sri Aurobindo's Philosophy* (Banares: Banares Hindu University, 1945), p. 127.

53. "Materialism," in *Supramental Manifestation*, 16: 247.

54. *Bande Mataram*, 1: 657-58. In *Foundations of Indian Culture*, vol. 14, Aurobindo criticizes the West for this emphasis on rationality that shows an absence of or at least shallow appreciation for spiritual knowledge and communion, a strength of the East.

55. *Bande Mataram*, 1: 655. See also "The Ideal of the Karmayogin" (*Kar-*

mayogin, 2: 19) where Aurobindo writes that Hinduism's "real, most authoritative scripture is in the heart in which the Eternal has His dwelling."

56. *Bande Mataram*, 1: 658.

57. *Ibid.*, p. 660. Bruteau points out that "the will of God" is Aurobindo's way of defining the purpose and destiny of human life. *World*, p. 266.

58. *Bande Mataram*, 1: 661-62.

59. *Ibid.*, p. 664.

60. According to Varma, this is definitely a new note in the traditions of Indian Vedanta to see the masses of people as the locus for the God-experience; he suggests that this position also provides a contrast to Europe, where "rationalism was based on common self-interest. In India it is based on the realization of God in the Motherland, devotion and love for the country" (*Political Philosophy*, p. 196). See also "The Glory of God in Man," in *Bande Mataram*, 1: 714-16.

61. "Uttarpara Speech," in *Karmayogin*, 2: 9-10.

62. *On Himself*, 26: 90-91.

63. See Langley, *Indian Poet*, pp. 24-30 on the limitations of the scientific method of knowledge; also *Life Divine*, 18: 6-16 on the materialist denial.

64. *On Himself*, 26: 91-92; for this reason he disclaims on p. 374 that he was ever a philosopher. On pp. 83-84 Aurobindo admits indebtedness to Lele, his guru during his Baroda days, although it becomes clear that he surpassed the need for a guru in his inclination to create his own yoga.

65. *Ibid.*, p. 181.

66. *Ibid.*, p. 125.

67. *Ibid.*, p. 221. As Bruteau suggests, it is evident here that Aurobindo speaks from within the darshana tradition, where knowing is seeing, having an intuitive experience of the reality—knowing it in becoming one with it. *World*, pp. 22-23.

68. *On Himself*, 26: 143. Chincholkar comments that while Aurobindo's insight about supermind is consonant with the Vedas and Upanishads, his understanding does not derive from them but from yogic realizations. *Critical Study*, p. 126.

69. Langley, *Indian Poet*, p. 46.

70. *Ibid.*, pp. 50-54.

3

The Meaning of Political Liberation

Political freedom is the life-breath of a nation; to attempt social reform, educational reform, industrial expansion, the moral improvement of the race without aiming first and foremost at political freedom, is the very height of ignorance and futility.[1]

In reading this statement originally published in 1907, we get a glimpse of Aurobindo's fundamental and unambiguous valuation of political freedom as the very life-breath of India. The radical issue for him is existence as a nation and he sees that the presence of the "white peril," Britain, was creating in India "imminent national death."[2] To achieve political freedom is to Aurobindo's mind identical with insuring the life of India. "Political freedom," "national freedom," "Swaraj"[3]— whatever the name, the issue is the very being of India as a people.

Aurobindo's appreciation for what is natural to the human spirit provides the framework for his perception: a nation's desire to grow from within and to exist out of its own strength is a "natural condition."[4] When such natural growth is interrupted by the intruding presence of a foreign power, all the

sources of nourishment and the natural centres . . . fail and disappear. It is for this reason that foreign rule can never be for the good of a nation, never work for its true progress and life, but must always work towards its disintegration and death.[5]

52

In order to insure its very "life-breath" and progress, India must return to its own natural sources and resourcefulness, tapping the life and strength that lie within, and that do not depend upon Britain nor upon any other external agent.[6]

Furthermore, Aurobindo's religious point of view pervades his approach to political freedom for India.[7] In "The New Faith" he warns the British bureaucracy that they are not hearing simply from a few frenetic leaders but from "a newly-awakened people to whom the political freedom of the country has been elevated to the height of a religious faith."[8] Throughout his speeches and editorials Aurobindo calls Indians to realize that they are engaged in a decision of vocation: to say no to the whims of the foreigner and yes to fulfilling a divinely appointed mission to the world. This mission is, as Aurobindo perceives it, "to supply the world with a perennial source of light and renovation . . . to organize life in the terms of Vedanta, . . . a work she cannot do while overshadowed by a foreign power and a foreign civilization."[9]

Aurobindo's confidence in the India of the holy Rishis, the India that bore Rama, Krishna, Buddha, and Guru Gobinda, prompts him to believe without hesitation that India is capable of such a mission.[10] This belief moves him to encourage his hearers to devote themselves, not in self-directed concern, but in service to the Motherland.[11]

Addressing himself to the masses, Aurobindo presents them with the challenging choice between two alternatives: India and freedom on the one hand, India and the bureaucracy on the other. At this point the lovers of freedom and the lovers of servitude speak their true loyalties—the moment reveals the difference between the wheat and the chaff.[12]

Speaking to the Moderates, Aurobindo criticizes the goals of the National Convention, which accepts colonial self-government *within* the British Empire instead of demanding full and total independence *from* the British Empire. With strong feeling and the rhetoric to express it, Aurobindo lashes out against this position:

> The degradation of a great nation, by the loss of her individuality, her past and her independent future, to the position of a subordinate satellite in a foreign system, is the ideal of the Convention. It is sheer political atheism, the negation of all that we were, are and hope to be.[13]

Rather, what Aurobindo and the nationalist position call for is the "return of India on her eternal self, the restoration of her splendour, greatness, triumphant Asiatic supremacy . . . ."[14] Indeed, nationalism is a creed and a religion; to be a nationalist means to enter the cause of the nation in a religious spirit and to see oneself as an instrument of God.[15]

> Nationalism survives in the strength of God and it is not possible to crush it, whatever weapons are brought against it. Nationalism is immortal; Nationalism cannot die; because it is no human thing; it is God who is working in Bengal. God cannot be killed, God cannot be sent to jail.[16]

Furthermore, Aurobindo maintains, those Bengali who suffered jail for their actions know that an almighty, invincible Power is guiding them and it is their task "to obey that Power," "to go where it leads them," "to speak the words that it tells them to speak and to do the thing that it tells them to do."[17]

Integral to this religious call to nationalism is Aurobindo's call to avoid the potential inclination of Indians to model themselves on Europe. European nationalism is for Aurobindo the replacement of "the dominion of the foreigner by the dominion of somebody else . . . a purely material change" that implies a desire not of freedom for one's countrymen, but a desire to rule others oneself.[18] India's vocation by contrast is to raise itself up in empathy with its three hundred millions and to make everyone share in the happiness of a newly felt freedom. What of the leaders of these masses? Are they not in danger of usurping power for the sake of prestige, dictation in lieu of direction? No. For to Aurobindo even the "leader" is described in terms of God's power within.

> The leader is within yourselves. If you can only find him and listen to his voice, then you will not find that people will not listen to you, because there will be a voice within the people which will make itself heard. That voice and that strength is within you. If you feel it within yourselves, if you live in its presence, if it has become yourselves, then you will find that one word from you will awake an answering voice in others, that the creed which you preach will spread and will be received by all.[19]

Such encouragement expresses a sharp contrast to India's former willingness to listen to the voice of Britain. In his analysis of the political maya that had bound India to live under the shackles of English education, English commerce, and English political systems, Aurobindo concludes that part of the horror of such bondage is rooted in the fact that the Indians participated in creating their own imprisonment by allowing England to so control them.

> We went to school with the aliens, we allowed the aliens to teach us and draw our minds away from all that was great and good in us. We considered ourselves unfit for self-government and political life, we looked to England as our exemplar and took her as our saviour.... We helped them to destroy what life there was in India... we ourselves became the instruments of our bondage.[20]

Thus, India allowed its self-dependence to dissolve. Yet, for Aurobindo a new moment had emerged from the suffering endured. The maya of the British presence broke open with Lord Curzon's partition of Bengal and then and there Indians began to discern that it was within their own power to make the "Swaraj within" real. Political freedom was then recognized as full independence from Britain.

Political Freedom: Independence (Swaraj)

Aurobindo's program for gaining political freedom became one of preaching "the gospel of unqualified Swaraj," encouraging India to realize that "free within is free without." This conviction moved Bhupen Dutt and Upadhyaya to refuse to make their case before a British court. Both are live historical models that Aurobindo points to to underscore his deep conviction that it is up to the Indians themselves to begin saying no to British repression. This would mean refusal to obey arbitrary laws designed to force India to conform to British convenience, unjustified charges of sedition and violence, and deportations.[21]

But this is not only a private hope of Aurobindo; he claims that such a call is in fact God's command: "God commands you to be free and you must be free."[22] Yet the close tie between the voice of God and the voice within are named when Aurobindo continues writing in the same paragraph:

> If you are true to yourself there is nothing to be afraid of . . . . It is not our work but that of something mightier that compels us to go on until all bondage is swept away and India stands free before the world.[23]

A more detailed study of Aurobindo's understanding indicates that swaraj functions for him as an "ideal" of "absolute autonomy free from foreign control" designed to foster India's self-dependence, strength, and sense of wholeness. His argument for swaraj as a value is based upon an appeal to nature, to history, and to his trust in the Indian people. The appeal to nature is evident in a claim that every nation has a "right . . . to live its own life by its own energies according to its own nature and ideals."[24] For Aurobindo this is a fundamental conviction and starting point. Subjection brings death (no matter how noble the subjecting party's motivation); only freedom nourishes life and makes growth viable.[25]

Aurobindo's appeal to history complements his appeal to nature. In brief, Aurobindo appeals to the experience of Britain's forcing an inferior civilization on India, thereby robbing the Indians of exploring their own roots and continuing the heritage of their past. The refusal to let this continue was to be motivated "not out of spite against the British, but in order to save our country."[26]

The appeal through trust in the people has already been named: Aurobindo is convinced of India's riches and resources and calls only for the opportunity for Indians to express themselves.[27]

> Our ideal of Swaraj involves no hatred of any other nation nor of the administration which is now established by law in this country. We find a bureaucratic administration, we wish to make it democratic; we find an alien government, we wish to make it indigenous; we find a foreign control, we wish to render it Indian . . . . We demand the realization of our corporate existence as a distinct race and nation because that is the only way in which the ultimate brotherhood of humanity can be achieved, not by blotting out individual peoples and effacing outward distinctions, but by removing the internal obstacles to unity, the causes of hatred, malice and misunderstanding.[28]

Swaraj demands that India begin reversing the process of foreign rule by constructing "its own organic centres of life and strength" as the India of the past had enjoyed in the "self-dependent village," in the central governing body, and in the Zemindar who linked the two.[29] Within his ever-present consciousness of growth, Aurobindo believes that India should restore the village in organizing swaraj in such a way that it can avoid isolation in its sense of self-sufficiency; his hope is that reconstruction will foster a feeling of being bound up with neighboring units under a common aspiration. Separatism has no place; shared life is the goal. And this shared life will be healthy only if the Indian "habit of subservience is removed and replaced by a habit of self-help."

> Our aim must be to revolutionise our habits and leave absolutely no corner of our life and activities in which the habit of dependence is allowed to linger or find refuge for its insidious and destructive working; education, commerce, industry, the administration of justice among ourselves, protection, sanitation, public works, one by one we must take them all back into our hands.[30]

In sum, self-help and self-dependence are the first conditions of swaraj.[31]

Second, Aurobindo responds to the need for consciousness-raising by focusing on the political sensibilities of all the people—not merely the few, the rulers, the learned, but the masses of Indians across the country.

> This is the age of the people, the millions, the democracy. If any nation wishes to survive in the modern struggle, if it wishes to recover or maintain Swaraj, it must awaken the people and bring them into the conscious life of the nation, so that every man may feel that in the nation he lives, with the prosperity of the nation he prospers, in the freedom of the nation he is free.[32]

Third, swaraj demands unity, a unity that is not limited to opinion, speech, or even intellectual conviction, but one that is rooted in the heart and prompted by love. Britain had survived on divisiveness rather than love, calling Indians away from mutual concern rather than nourishing ties of affection. But Aurobindo felt that the Indian village would be able to "destroy the aloofness, the separateness of our lives and . . . restore the lost sense of brotherhood" through meeting water needs, relieving medical and famine needs, establishing arbitration courts, and protecting just rights.[33] In sum, "political freedom is but a limb of Swarajya, self-empire."[34]

To this ideal of swaraj as described, Aurobindo invites his hearers to vow themselves.[35] For the fundamental purpose of the swaraj movement is "the fulfilment [of India] . . . as a nation,"[36] fulfillment that will touch the life of the individual, the life of the family, the life of the community, the life of the nation, eventually the life of humanity itself.[37] For Aurobindo such "fulfilment is life [itself] and to depart from it is to perish."[38]

In a key speech, "The Right of Association," given June 27, 1909, Aurobindo unearths the inherent right within a nation to unify. It is the right of association that he feels is the "sign and safeguard of liberty and means of development of a common life." Detailing this observation, Aurobindo alludes to the three characteristic rights enjoyed and demanded by free nations. First, there is "the right of a free Press," which insures the power most responsible for a people's development, "the power of spreading the idea." Aurobindo continues, "according to our philosophy it is the idea which is building up the world" and is the primary agent of change.[39] Second, "the right of public meeting" occurs when people are bound by common hopes and impulses and tend to cohere in order to share and support one another in these movements. Third, "the right of association" provides the instrument to translate the ideas and the inclinations into actions, converting rhetoric into practical politics.[40]

Yet, association is not the structure of an organization with its chairperson, assistant, and secretary; it is rather a "feeling" and a "force": a feeling of brotherhood, the force of love, of common bonds for a common work; it is the spirit of selflessness and self-sacrifice.[41] In fact, it is "the mightiest thing in humanity; it is the instrument by which humanity moves; it is the means by which it progresses towards its final development."[42]

This right of association has found expression in what have become known as the three values of liberty, equality, and fraternity, which indicate the human thrust toward the evolutionary goals. And it is these three values that are threatened by a government unwilling to change with the needs of the moment. Aurobindo sensed that the mood of the moment was thick with such unwillingness on the part of Britain; this indicated to him that these ideals expressed both the hope that sustained India and the contradiction that was Europe—a complex of countries that deprived others of the very freedoms and rights they had fought for themselves.

The freedom Aurobindo was seeking was not only a freedom from bondage to Britain, but also a lost preexistent freedom religiously envisioned. In seeking such original liberty or ultimate emancipation, the Indians would be seeking and achieving freedom of the soul, which he designates as freedom of the body too, freedom of the whole person. Granting Europe's attainment of external freedom, Aurobindo claims that India's most precious prize will be the internal freedom that characterizes its history. Britain and India need to learn from each other's struggle: Britain can learn to aspire after internal freedom as India has learned to aspire after external freedom.

His reflections on equality indicate once again his religious world view as he remembers that Hinduism claims equality to be the essential condition of liberation. In fact, Aurobindo sees equality to be the common theme of all religions, whether it be imaged in terms of the brotherhood of men and the children of God, or the subjects and servants of Allah, or the oneness of all persons and things. Unless a person lives as well as sees this equality, one is not free.

Fraternity appears as the most difficult to achieve, yet is undoubtedly what people aspire to continually. Fraternity means brotherhood and peace and love; it is the modern gospel of humanitarianism as well as the ancient gospels of Jesus and the Buddha. This desire is rooted in the very nature of humanity and indicates an innate reluctance to live in isolation. In spite of conflict, struggle, and discord, the human community continues its attempt to achieve fraternity.[43]

Of the three ideals of liberty, equality, and fraternity, considered within the gestalt of a single design, Aurobindo criticizes the French for underestimating the importance of the last. He considers their revolution a failure on the basis that, because France was so concerned with gaining social and political liberty and equality, the French revolutionaries did not sufficiently value fraternity. Without fraternity the establishment of social equality is not possible: "Fraternity is the basis of equality . . . . Only brotherly feeling can bring about brotherhood." [44]

These values indicate Aurobindo's concern with ideals as well as with political maneuverings. Although political concerns and strategies are ever present in Aurobindo's image of the future, and we will consider these next, it must be remembered that these questions are always placed within the context of his overarching religious vision. For, in his words, there is

> one entity which we believe to be all-important, the *dharma*, the national religion which we also believe to be universal. There is a mighty law of life, a great principle of human evolution, a body of spiritual knowledge and experience of which India has always been destined to be guardian, exemplar and missionary. This is the *sanatāna dharma*, the eternal religion. [45]

Yet, given his political concerns at this time, what strategies and goals mark Aurobindo's early thought? By what means does he hope to achieve political liberation?

Means and Ends

Regarding the question about the means by which political freedom is to be achieved, it is clear from his speeches that Aurobindo values a method of confrontation rather than withdrawal. "It is by looking the storm in the face and meeting it with a high courage, fortitude and endurance that the nation can be saved." [46] This approach of confrontation is expressed in basically two complementary ways: self-help and passive resistance. [47]

Self-help demands a habit of free thought and action at the national level as well as a clearly organized authority, such as the Nationalist Party, which functions to give direction and leadership throughout the entire nation. As a motivating principle, self-help depends for its fruitfulness upon the willingness of the people to fear social excommunication by their own peers far more deeply than censure by a foreign rule; it depends on a strong ability to bear inconvenience and suffering; it depends upon a determined endurance that is far beyond what is needed in either normal military revolt or in revolution; and it depends on the decisions of the British bureaucracy not to interfere with the nonviolent and constructive projects of Indian educational, industrial, and legislative efforts.[48]

Yet, it is because bureaucratic opposition is expected as the British response to India's commitment to self-help that Aurobindo is quickly ushered into a consideration of the second means to political freedom: "passive" or "defensive resistance."[49] For only by organized Indian resistance will self-development be effected.[50]

Whether resistance itself be expressed passively or aggressively, whether people deliberately abstain from helping the government or bring about positive harm to the government through armed revolt,[51] is a matter to be decided on the basis of circumstances. Aurobindo's assessment of the India of his day leads him to call for the use of passive resistance as the "most natural and suitable weapon." He makes it very clear that this decision is not based on any unchanging ethical principles nor on the absolutization of nonviolence. History tells him that the very "conscience of humanity" approves of bloodshed and violence and that "the morality of war is different from the morality of peace."[52]

Aurobindo's position on violence and war can be derived, in part at least, from his reading of the Gita, which names the war of Kurukshetra to be a "righteous war" because Sri Krishna was attempting through it "to destroy the Kurus, to destroy the power of the Kshatriyas, to establish an undisputed imperial authority and the unity of India."[53] In order to offset a national calamity, fighting in war becomes not a sin but a duty; in Kurukshetra, God saved India.[54]

Since liberty is the life-breath of the nation for Aurobindo, any means taken to preserve that life, in the face of violent pressure to suppress it, becomes right and justifiable—just as it is right and justifiable for a single person to resist a strangler by any means available. He continues:

> It is the nature of the pressure which determines the nature of the resistance . . . . Where the need for immediate liberty is urgent and it is a present question of national life or death on the instant, revolt is the only course. But where the oppression is legal and subtle in its

methods and respects life, liberty and property and there is still breathing time, the circumstances demand that we should make the experiment of a method of resolute but peaceful resistance.[55]

The style of decision-making on the basis of effects, results, consequences, presents a dilemma regarding Aurobindo's theoretical stance. Aurobindo justifies the war of Kurukshetra in terms of the need to establish authority and unity in India. Here the desired authority and unity, two hoped-for consequences (or "fruits") of the conflict, determine the legitimacy of participation in the conflict. The events of Aurobindo's own life also indicate that he espoused revolutionary strategies precisely in terms of the efficacy of these results (fruits). And yet, in his "Introduction to the Gita," Aurobindo underscores with approval the Gita's message that one should renounce and be detached from the fruit or results of one's actions and be concerned only with the nature of the act: "one should not look to the fruit of works, one has to decide whether a particular act is right or wrong by looking into its nature."[56] How may we interpret this inconsistency?

One interpretation might be that Aurobindo was simply unable to translate into practice his understanding of the Gita. But another interpretation suggests itself as a possibility: that there is no inconsistency here at all, that obviously to choose political strategies detached from their results would be self-defeating and therefore absurd; that what the Gita is talking about is of a completely different order; that the order of the one is sociopolitical and historical, the other inner-personal and spiritual; that the political struggle demands by definition the achievement of power and position, whereas the egoless union with Brahman depends upon detachment from power and position.

In conversation with Purani in 1939 regarding the inherent limitations of Gandhi's tactics, Aurobindo faults Gandhi for "trying to apply to ordinary life what belongs to spirituality,"[57] suggesting that "ordinary life" and "spirituality" are two quite different orders and that consistency between them should not be expected. But to develop this point further is to anticipate the final discussion of the study, a discussion that focuses more explicitly upon the nature of the relationship between the political and the spiritual in Aurobindo's life and thought.

Organized refusal to help Britain—in commerce or government—is the first principle of passive resistance. This is best captured in the practice of boycott, which is the systematic attempt to immobilize Britain by refusing to buy British goods, refusing to send Indian children to government schools, refusing to plead before British courts of law, refusing to seek help from or allow interference by the executive arm of Britain.[58] In a word, boycott said to the British: "no control, no assistance."[59]

This slogan, plus the strong endorsement Aurobindo gave to the strategies of political, economic, and social boycott, touches the question of law and its place in Aurobindo's thought. As has been hinted at thus far, Aurobindo's regard for the law is serious yet qualified, both reverent and relative.

In one of his early essays on the spiritual basis of the universe, "The Stress of the Hidden Spirit," he unfolds his fundamental perception of law as identical with the nature of things, as simply the way things are. Whereas evolution is a term used to describe a process sequence, the recurring question of "why" cannot be adequately handled by the evolutionary perspective alone. The question of origin remains—how account for the process of evolution itself?

> Why should the seed produce a tree and not some other form of existence? The answer is, because that is its nature. But why is that its nature? Why should it not be its nature to produce some other form of existence, or some other kind of tree? That is the law, is the answer. But why is it the law? The only answer is that it is so because it is so; that it happens, why, no man can say.[60]

Identifying the law of a thing with the nature of that thing, Aurobindo continues his response to the question of "why" by then identifying law and nature with an idea. "The seed evolves a tree because the tree is the idea involved in the seed; it is a process of manifestation in form, not a creation." Without such an "insistent idea" manifested by "an originating and ordering intelligence," the only alternative for Aurobindo would be "a world of chances and freaks, not a world of law."[61]

This law of nature is elsewhere identified with *dharma*, the divine law;

it is described as the right law of life, the way of action and the way of abstention—whatever is not marred by self-interest, but is consecrated to the divine, be it politics, poetry, or painting.[62]

In addition to Aurobindo's perception of and respect for the natural law of the universe or the divine law manifested in the universe, there is a respect for the law of the nation as well. Such respect, according to Aurobindo, has always characterized the Indian people and is a crucial factor in the endurance of any nation. Consequently he encouraged scrupulous observance of the law, yet one that was neither naive nor absolutist. For he also encouraged his people to take "every advantage both of the protection it gives and the latitude it still leaves for pushing forward our cause and our propaganda."[63]

On this issue of latitude within the law, Aurobindo legitimates boycott strategies and alternative means of noncooperation since these tactics are designed not to destroy the law through aggressive resistance, but to recall the law by means of organized disobedience. To Aurobindo a law that is constituted by aliens and imposed on a people from without does not have the binding quality of a law that a people imposes upon itself. Such an exteriorly imposed law is dependent upon coercive control or on its own good character, but is not dependent on its source.

To resist such laws is to make this utterly clear to the law-maker. Aurobindo is convinced that his ideal is one that no man-made law can condemn and that his methods are those which no civilized government, in honesty and humanity, can declare illegal.[64] His purpose is not to break the law; his purpose is to disestablish, through peaceful though resolute means, those repressive laws which deny the law of progress,[65] and thereby invite refusal to succumb. For "to break an unjust coercive law is not only justifiable but, under given circumstances, a duty."[66]

Always the insistence is on active response. And much of the reason behind this current is Aurobindo's esteem for the quality of aggression as characteristic of the India of old, and as intrinsic to the power of self-preservation. Without aggressive self-preservation life ceases.[67]

In this spirit India grounds its strength, for India cannot point to any material strengths—there are no armaments, indigenous education, or national government. Yet India has a tradition of soul-force, deep and full within its history, and this is the strength to be tapped now.[68]

This preference for a peaceful expression of aggression as a means of revolutionary change is in no way derived from any absolute principle. Aurobindo chose peaceful strategies because of the practical circumstances of the moment and he was fully aware of the limits of passive resistance. "So long as the action of the executive is peaceful and within the rules of the fight, the passive resister scrupulously maintains his attitude of passivity, but he is not bound to do so a moment beyond." Not only is he not expected to submit to illegal or violent coercion, but to do so is "to sin against the divinity within" and "the divinity in [the] motherland." At such a moment "active resistance becomes a duty." [69]

Another limitation to passive resistance resides in human experience itself and its tolerance for endurance. In moments or situations when such tolerance is tested in outrageous expressions of tyranny, the choice becomes one of two things: "to break under the strain and go under or to throw it off with violence." [70]

Passive resistance, though the preferred method of refusal, is to be employed only as it truly helps the nationalist cause in achieving national freedom. [71] It becomes pointless to make an ethical absolute of something that is really chosen for pragmatic value. In fact,

It is a barren philosophy which applies a mechanical rule to all actions, or takes a word and tries to fit all human life into it.

The sword of the warrior is as necessary to the fulfilment of justice and righteousness as the holiness of the saint. [72]

In a word, the means by which political freedom is achieved is chosen because the circumstances of the time indicate that passive resistance will be the most fruitful; passive resistance will work best in the here and now. But what about this question of means? Is political freedom a means to some end? Or is it an end in itself?

Aurobindo speaks of the political freedom he worked for as a "condition of self-fulfilment"; [73] he also suggests that it is a means to attain the goal of "building up India for the sake of humanity . . . . For that work the freedom and greatness of India are essential . . . ." [74]

In this position regarding the relationship of freedom and unity, Aurobindo fought hard against the moderate position as expressed in *The Bengalee*, edited by a well-known moderate leader, Surendranath Bannerjee. Editorials in *The Bengalee* argued that unity was a value to be considered an end in itself, identical with progress, freedom, and greatness. In sharp contrast to this reading, Aurobindo argues that unity makes sense only if freedom has been its foundation. "It is not true that unity, even political unity, is identical with freedom, for a nation may be united in bondage or united in submission to a foreign and absolutist rule." [75]

The national unity Aurobindo envisions can come about only when India's life-center comes from within itself and not from an alien, external source. His vision of India's "Heaven-appointed mission" [76] as the ultimate religious goal, and as dependent upon India's own sense of strength and self-determination, further supports Aurobindo's conviction that freedom is indeed a means.

The end then becomes politicoreligious: India's right to self-rule, and India's mission to call all of humanity to realize the spiritual nature of the universe and the all-pervading unifying presence of the divine. [77] For Aurobindo both freedom and unity are essential political gains. One alone is incomplete. [78]

In this consideration of political freedom it must be sharply recognized that Aurobindo is also continuously conscious of another dimension of freedom, spiritual freedom perhaps, or what he frequently calls "inner freedom" or "the freedom of the inner life." [79]

Spiritual Freedom

As mentioned in chapter 1, Aurobindo began the practice of yoga during his Baroda days and found that the Alipore jail provided further opportunity to explore the world of yoga. There he discovered that the perennial political and social search of a people to gain freedom is also true on the level of the individual. While the paths are many (renunciation, control, epicureanism, Buddhism, yoga), the goal is the same: the "freedom of the inner life." [80]

Aurobindo criticizes the claim put forward in psychological and biological theories that freedom is an illusion. He maintains that

the longing to be free is lodged in such a deep layer of the human heart that a thousand arguments are helpless to uproot it. Man can never remain content with the conclusions of the physical sciences. In all ages he has felt vaguely that the subtle elements capable of conquering the physical limits are definitely to be found in his own inner being, that there is an Inner Controller, a Person, for ever free and full of Delight, within him.[81]

Furthermore, Aurobindo names the goal of "eternal freedom" as the object of spiritual seeking encouraged in religion and as the object of evolutionary development spoken of by science. This state is concretized in the Gita's description of the ideal person: one who "renounces the desire for the fruit of action and practices active renunciation in the supreme Person, Purushottama."[82] Within the bounds of the Alipore jail, Aurobindo met men who possessed this detachment, Nagendra and Dharani, examples of the little people often overlooked by the educated, yet strikingly deep, full, free persons in spite of their prison walls.[83]

Traditionally it has been held that the goal of the Hindu religion is "emancipation from the bondage of material Nature and freedom from individual rebirth." In contrast to this, Aurobindo's intent is to emphasize Krishna's stress on the perfect yogi remaining involved in human life and exchange, doing good as a vessel of divine power or as a leader in the forefront of the action itself.[84]

This quest for "self-liberation"[85] or freedom of the inner self involves two major movements. First, one must break through the illusion of agency and realize that nature and not the self is the cause of action. Second, one must surrender oneself to the divine.

The context for the first demand is a philosophic position that claims that all being has a two-fold reality: Purusha (soul or conscious being) and Prakriti (nature or universal energy). Prakriti is the true agent in life, directing developments according to the law of cause and effect. The soul is not the agent but that which enjoys the result of the action of Prakriti, which is nature.[86] We become victim to the illusion that we are agents when we forget and so identify ourselves with Prakriti as to lose the sense of our distinction from Prakriti.[87]

Aurobindo developed the issue of freedom in an article, "Fate and Free-Will,"[88] in which he frames the question in terms of the relationship between the human being and the Power (whether intelligent or unintelligent) that rules the world. We seem to be free; we seem to do what we choose to do. The question, however, is: is it possible that this sense of freedom is in fact illusory and that our apparent freedom is really a bondage? Are we in truth bound by the will of a supreme intelligent power? (That is, are we predestined?) Or are we bound by blind nature? Or by the necessity of a previous development?

Addressing himself to each of these three questions and their correlative theories, Aurobindo feels that unless one adopts a "Calvinistic Fatalism" there is no intrinsic incompatibility between the coexistence of an overriding divine will and freedom of the individual. As for the determinism of blind nature, Aurobindo places this theory in the world of the scientist, who finds the word *freedom* empty of meaning due to a discovery of the many determinisms of nature. As for the third theory, the necessity of one's previous development, Aurobindo assigns this interpretation to Buddhistic and post-Buddhistic Hinduism, which he claims is a misreading of the theory of karma.

Genuine Hindu teaching, however, independent of Buddhistic influence, expresses a view of human life that recognizes both fate and free will. For Aurobindo fate means an "insistent causality which is only another name for Law, and Law itself is only an instrument in the hands of Nature for the satisfaction of the spirit." Law here is *dharma* and means "holding together," functioning as it does to unify the action of the universe and its parts, and the action of the individual. This action is what is known as karma, so *dharma* or law comes to mean "action as decided by the nature of the thing in which action takes place." The individual acts according to its nature, the group according to its nature, the universe according to its nature.

> The whole of causality may be defined as previous action leading to subsequent action, *karma* and *karmaphala*. The Hindu theory is that thought and feeling, as well as actual speech or deeds, are part of *karma* and create effect.[89]

What saves this interpretation from determinism without escape is that "there is something within us which is free and Lord, superior to Nature." And this is spirit, "ever free and blissful . . .one in essence and in reality with the Supreme Soul of the Universe." Yet Aurobindo is clear in stating that it is not the spirit that acts, for if the spirit acted it would be bound by its action; rather it is nature, Prakriti, that acts and determines the nature of things and "is the source and condition of Law." [90]

In other words, Aurobindo perceives that the soul sustains the nature, "watches" and "enjoys" the action, and "sanctions" the law, giving consent as does a king; yet, like the king, this spirit or soul remains above the law and free. Free will, then, consists in the individual soul's power of sanction to affirm what the supreme soul or will allows Prakriti to do. "This is the great truth now dawning on the world, that Will is the thing which moves the world and that Fate is merely a process by which Will fulfils itself." [91]

In order then for the individual soul to feel its own power to direct life's events, it must become one with the infinite and universal spirit, identifying its will with the universal will. Actual freedom of the soul comes with the individual's conscious surrender to the universal will. [92] This points to the second movement toward self-liberation.

As the soul dissolves the illusion of its own agency, the process of liberation is furthered by "surrendering lordship to God, leaving Him alone to uphold and sanction by the abdication of one's own independent use of these powers." When "the *sāksī* or witness withdraws into God Himself, that is the utter liberation." [93] But yoga is more than the individual's entry into liberation; though necessarily involving more time, yoga is also necessary for humanity in order that the next step in human evolution be taken. [94]

What precisely does yoga do for a person? It enables one to analyze experiences of both mind and heart and thus to discover a "primal spiritual entity from which all proceeds" together with a "psychical centre" that enables the yogi "to fix the roots of personality." [95] The discoveries resulting are basically four: first, that the mind can isolate itself from objects and thus become capable of working in and of itself; second, that the more detached from objects the mind becomes, the more powerfully and clearly it can work; third, that these mental phenomena proceed by laws of their own and are independent of those thought processes which act upon matter; fourth, that mind is the master of matter, and

can not only reject and control external stimuli, but can defy such apparently universal material laws as that of gravitation and ignore, put aside and make nought of what are called laws of nature and are really only the laws of material nature, inferior and subject to the psychical laws because matter is a product of mind and not mind a product of matter.[96]

Whatever the theory, "the progress of humanity is a fact,"[97] and it is the task of humankind to participate in the continuation of that progress. The thrust of evolution for Aurobindo is the growth by which the brute love of oneself becomes increasingly overtaken by love for others. In this way the "narrow self" becomes taken over by an "everlasting self," and moral growth is fostered.[98] Evolution will be fulfilled when the individual selves find, in knowledge, love, and action, communion and identity with the universal self, which is God. This goal is *mukti*. In the past, morality and religion have achieved conquest of the body and the vital self and thus played a key role in the furtherance of human evolution. But the conquest of emotion and intellect by the spirit remains the work to be accomplished in the future. "Yoga is the means by which that conquest becomes possible."[99]

It is known that we can alter the associations of mind and body temporarily and that the mind can alter the conditions of the body partially. Yoga asserts that these things can be done permanently and completely. For the body, conquest of disease, pain and material obstructions, for the mind, liberation from bondage to past experience and the heavier limitations of space and time, for the heart victory over sin and grief and fear, for the spirit unclouded bliss, strength and illumination, this is the gospel of Yoga, this is the goal to which Hinduism points humanity.[100]

And this is the goal toward which Aurobindo strove in his own personal struggle to integrate the political and the spiritual.

The Struggle toward Integration

Aurobindo's essays reveal what he saw to be a necessary relationship of interaction between the political and the spiritual; a passage from the *Karmayogin* reflects this with respect to his concern for freedom. "It is the spirit alone that saves, and only by becoming great and free in heart can we become socially and politically great and free."[101]

His theoretical positions reflect his lived experience. For during his politically active period, Aurobindo was deepening his practice of yoga and openness to spiritual experience. Both the "Prison Experiences"[102] and the "Uttarpara Speech"[103] give witness to this as autobiographical accounts of how Aurobindo's personal commitment to political freedom touched levels of life within him that he experienced as deeply spiritual as well.

These experiences then prompted him to call his people to the same conviction and commitment to which he sensed he was called by Krishna:

> When you go forth, speak to your nation always this word, that it is for the Sanatan Dharma that they arise, it is for the world and not for themselves that they arise. I am giving them freedom for the service of the world.[104]

This movement from freedom for India to freedom for the world was to become the pattern in Aurobindo's own life-style and it is timely now to turn our attention to what this larger spiritual freedom meant to him and what he felt were its ingredients and implications. First, however, it seems wise to review the findings of chapter 3 and state summarily the way Aurobindo's works answer the questions posed.

Summary

We have found that Aurobindo grounds the value of political freedom within the value of existence itself, claiming that political freedom is the very life-breath of the nation. Consequently, political freedom is prerequisite to any avenue of evolutionary growth, whether industrial, educational, social, or moral, and his call to political freedom consistently appeals to the religious sensibilities of the Indian people. The context for valuing their independence is in terms of a *creed* expressed in a *mission* of *service* to shed "*eternal light*"[105] and "*save* the whole world.*"[106] The people are asked to *vow* faith, selflessness, and courage, through which they are better able to follow *God's command* to realize the *gospel* of unqualified swaraj and thus achieve the "fulfilment of the Vedantic ideal in politics."[107]

Political freedom means radical independence from Britain and from things European, in government, of course, but also in consciousness and life-style. The Indian people are to rediscover and to tap the resources of their own rich heritage as they regain their self-dependence, saying no to domination from without, no to dependence on forces from without. The means of saying no include openness to insurrection and armed revolt, yet in effect, for contextual reasons, emphasize procedures of passive resistance (through economic, educational, judicial boycott) and self-help (positive programs for developing indigenous economic, educational, and judicial structures).

Valuable as political freedom is for Aurobindo, he sees it as a condition and starting point rather than as final goal or completion. Always his perspective enlarges to a freedom beyond that of political freedom, a freedom he names "inner freedom," what we might call the larger human freedom for all people. The political freedom of India is a necessary step in the total process, but Aurobindo never forgets that it is precisely that: a step. Unity among nations and unity of all people with the Supreme Spirit is the final goal on which his hopes and his vision are fixed.

For it is only in this perspective that people can discover that their lives are marked not merely by freedom of will or choice, but that their lives are also marked by fate, by the determining will of an intelligent supreme existence. The individual's deepest freedom, for Aurobindo in his early days, consists in surrendering to the divine and thereby realizing that the source of action is Prakriti or nature's universal energy and not the self; and that while the supreme spirit remains above and free from such action, he enjoys, watches, and sanctions what Prakriti does. Yoga is the recommended means to achieve this surrender and is not only available to the individual but is necessary for humankind as a whole if evolution is to be fulfilled.

Given the initial methodological format in which this study has been framed, it can now be stated that Aurobindo's participation in the political arena and his personal pursuits into yoga constitute the experiential base of concretely lived moments and events. These experiences precipitated his position with respect to the meaning and value of political and personal (inner, spiritual) freedom discussed in this chapter. These interpretations and valuations in turn have prompted Aurobindo to recommend strategies for action: self-help and resistance for the achievement of political freedom; yogic discipline and concentration for the achievement of inner freedom (both individually and collectively).

Aurobindo's involvement in the political struggle, together with his yogic pursuits, indicates the politicospiritual nature of his early concerns and provides the setting out of which he later develops at Pondicherry a fuller understanding of spiritual freedom or inner freedom. To this issue and this period of his life we now turn.

Notes

1. "The Doctrine of Passive Resistance" (1907), in *Bande Mataram*, 1:86. See also "The Unhindu Spirit of Caste Rigidity" (September 20, 1907), in *Bande Mataram*, 1:535, where Aurobindo indicates that political freedom is a necessary condition for meeting other needs crucial to Indian life, such as economic reconstruction, education, and social change.

2. "Doctrine of Passive Resistance," in *Bande Mataram*, 1:96.

3. *Ibid.*, p. 118.

4. "Palli Samiti" (speech, 1908), in *Bande Mataram*, 1:884.

5. *Ibid.*

6. This respect for the within is also reflected in Aurobindo's educational theory, where he emphasizes that the mind must be consulted in its own growth and invited to discover, never imposed upon. See "The Human Mind" (1909-10), in *The Hour of God*, 17:204-5.

7. David L. Johnson has written a dissertation on precisely this theme. See *Aurobindo Ghose and Indian Nationalism: A Religious Analysis* (University of Iowa, 1972). The manuscript has also been published under a new title: *The Religious Roots of Indian Nationalism: Aurobindo's Early Political Thought* (Calcutta: Firma K. L. Mukhopadhyay, 1974).

8. (November 30, 1907) in *Bande Mataram*, 1:613.

9. "Ideals Face to Face" (May 1, 1908), in *Bande Mataram*, 1:903.

10. "The New Faith" (1907), in *Bande Mataram*, 1:613; also "The New Ideal" (April 7, 1908), in *Bande Mataram*, 1:836.

11. See "Advice to National College Students" (Speech, 1907), in *Bande Mataram*, 1:515-17.

12. "The Wheat and the Chaff" (April 23, 1908), in *Bande Mataram*, 1:870-74.

13. "Ideals Face to Face" (1908), in *Bande Mataram*, 1:904. For a study in the contrasting positions between the Moderates and the Nationalists (Extremists), see Daniel Argov, *Moderates and Extremists in the Indian Nationalist Movement 1883-1920* (New York: Asia Publishing House, 1967).

14. *Ibid.*

15. "The Present Situation" (speech delivered January 19, 1908), in *Bande Mataram*, 1: 652-53.

16. *Ibid.*, p. 653.

17. *Ibid.*, p. 660. As evident from the "Uttarpara Speech" (delivered May 30, 1909), quoted in chap. 2 of this study, this was exactly Aurobindo's own experience during his imprisonment. His experience of Krishna transformed his consciousness and he henceforth saw the divine everywhere. See *Karmayogin*, 2: 1-10 for the entire text. See also "Tales of Prison Life," *Sri Aurobindo Mandir Annual*, no. 27 (August 15, 1968), p. 139. A letter to his wife Mrinalini, dated August 30, 1905, indicates, however, that Aurobindo had already sensed then that he was sent to earth by God and that his mission was to fight not with guns and the force of the Kshatriya but with knowledge and the force of the Brahmin. *Sri Aurobindo Mandir Annual*, no. 26 (August 15, 1967), p. 119.

18. "The Present Situation," in *Bande Mataram*, 1: 662.

19. *Ibid.*, p. 664.

20. "Baruipur Speech" (delivered April 12, 1908), in *Bande Mataram*, 1: 856. See also "Doctrine of Passive Resistance," in *Bande Mataram*, 1: 99. Another essay pertinent to this topic is "The Problem of the Past" (1908), trans. Niranjan, *Sri Aurobindo Mandir Annual*, no. 26 (August 15, 1967), pp. 96-101, where Aurobindo deals with the question: why did England have the power to so control India? His answer is that "though the Indians were equal to the English in all qualities, they did not have any national feeling whereas the English possessed it to the full" (*ibid.*, p. 97). And "the lack of national consciousness was a more fatal defect than the lack of unity" (*ibid.*, p. 98).

21. "Baruipur Speech" (1908), in *Bande Mataram*, 1: 857. See also "Jhalakati Speech" (delivered June 19, 1909), in *Karmayogin*, 2: 57-66. It is pertinent here to note that even while Aurobindo is decrying the unjustified suffering Britain has imposed upon India, he sees suffering itself as the action of God calling India to new life. "Repression is nothing but the hammer of God that is beating us into shape so that we may be moulded into a mighty nation and an instrument for his work in the world . . . . Without suffering there can be no growth" (*ibid.*, pp. 61-62). See also "Beadon Square Speech" (1909), in *Karmayogin*, 2: 25, where Aurobindo sees the national suffering as a "price" India "had to pay for its previous lapses from national duty."

22. "Baruipur Speech" (1908), in *Bande Mataram*, 1: 857. See also references to "God's law" in "Beadon Square Speech," in *Karmayogin*, 2: 25-28.

23. "Baruipur Speech," in *Bande Mataram*, 1: 857-58.

24. *"An Open Letter to My Countrymen" (July 31, 1909),* in *Karmayogin*, 2: 126.

25. "The True Meaning of Freedom" (1909), trans. Niranjan, *Sri Aurobindo Mandir Annual*, no. 26 (August 15, 1967), pp. 104-5.

26. *Ibid.*, p. 105.

27. "An Open Letter to My Countrymen" (1909), in *Karmayogin*, 2: 126. See also "The Ideal of the Karmayogin," in *Karmayogin*, 2: 20, where he writes, "It is God's will that we should be ourselves and not Europe."

28. "An Open Letter to My Countrymen," in *Karmayogin*, 2: 126-27.

29. "Palli Samiti," in *Bande Mataram*, 1: 884.

30. *Ibid.*, pp. 885-86.

31. *Ibid.*, p. 886.

32. *Ibid.* In his "Introduction to the Gita" (1909-10), *Sri Aurobindo Mandir Annual*, no. 27 (August 15, 1968), p. 93, Aurobindo criticizes India for her lack of political awareness; he feels that although such teaching can be found in the Gita, the Mahabharata, and other ancient sources, India neglected to pay attention to this theme of political awareness and eventually it "had to be imported from the West."

33. "Palli Samiti," in *Bande Mataram*, 1: 887-88.

34. "The True Meaning of Freedom" (1909), trans. Niranjan, *Sri Aurobindo Mandir Annual*, no. 26 (August 15, 1967), p. 104.

35. "Palli Samiti," in *Bande Mataram*, 1: 888.

36. "Jhalakati Speech" (1909), in *Karmayogin*, 2: 63.

37. *Ibid.*, p. 64. See also "The Ideal of the Karmayogin," in *Karmayogin*, 2: 19, where Aurobindo unequivocally sets the role of India within the context of humanity: "Our aim will therefore be to help in building up India for the sake of humanity—this is the spirit of Nationalism which we profess and follow." See also "Introduction to the Gita," *Sri Aurobindo Mandir Annual*, no. 27 (August 15, 1968), p. 92.

38. "Jhalakati Speech," in *Karmayogin*, 2: 64.

39. In *Karmayogin*, 2: 81.

40. *Ibid.*, pp. 82-83.

41. *Ibid.*, p. 94. In "The Doctrine of Sacrifice," in *Karmayogin*, 2: 107, Aurobindo unfolds his esteem for this virtue by naming it not a characteristic common to all men nor all nations, but a "genius . . . rare and precious . . . the flowering of mankind's ethical growth, the evidence of our gradual rise from the self-regarding animal to the selfless divinity." To give oneself for one's mate, one's children, one's community, one's nation reveals the movement that self-sacrifice takes. The highest form is the willingness to give up oneself to all humanity—an act most people are not yet capable of doing, but hopefully are moving toward. *Ibid.*, p. 108.

42. "Right of Association," in *Karmayogin*, 2: 83.

43. *Ibid.*, pp. 83-85. It is impossible to listen seriously to Aurobindo on this topic without questioning whether or not he ever questioned these values of liberty, fraternity, and particularly, equality, with respect to the caste system. His observations reflect both criticism and justification of the caste structure. In "The Right of Association," in *Karmayogin*, 2: 85, he writes that though admittedly marked with numerous defects, the caste system was "an attempt, however imperfect, to base society upon the principle of association, the principle of closely organising a common life founded on common ideas, common feelings, common tendencies, a common moral discipline and sense of corporate honour." Because of the "moral deterioration and material decay," these bonds have been severed and the spirit behind the caste system has dissolved. Without the spirit, the form has necessarily broken apart.

Nonetheless, without the distinct caste contributions, India would be less that it is. For India needs the spirituality and knowledge of the Brahmin, the manhood and strength of the Kshatriya, the industry and thrift of the Vaishya, and the simplicity and labor of the Shudra ("Ourselves" [1909] in *Karmayogin*, 2: 11-13). See also "Introduction to the Gita," *Sri Aurobindo Mandir Annual*, no. 27 (August 15, 1968), p. 19. Applying this to the individual, Aurobindo claims that the true yogi expands himself to include all of these traits and thus achieve the fullness of integral perfection (*Synthesis of Yoga*, 21: 712-23). Other pertinent references include "Tales of Prison Life" (1909-10), *Sri Aurobindo Mandir Annual*, no. 27 (August 15, 1968), p. 130, and "To My Countrymen," in *Karmayogin*, 2: 327.

44. "Fraternity" (1910), trans. Niranjan, *Sri Aurobindo Mandir Annual*, no. 26 (August 15, 1967), p. 107.

45. "Ideal of the Karmayogin," in *Karmayogin*, 2: 17.

46. "Jhalakati Speech," in *Karmayogin*, 2: 65.

47. "College Square Speech" (1909), in *Karmayogin*, 2: 114-15. Also "An Open Letter to My Countrymen," in *Karmayogin*, 2: 127. In "Doctrine of Passive Resistance," in *Bande Mataram*, 1: 85, Aurobindo names petitioning as another possible policy, though he immediately rejects it as totally unrealistic at that point in history.

48. *Ibid.*, pp. 87-88. See also "College Square Speech," in *Karmayogin*, 2: 114.

49. "Doctrine of Passive Resistance," in *Bande Mataram*, 1: 89.

50. *Ibid.*, pp. 95-96.

51. *Ibid.*, p. 101.

52. *Ibid.*, pp. 97-98.

53. "Introduction to the Gita," *Sri Aurobindo Mandir Annual*, no. 27 (August 15, 1968), p. 96. See also *Essays on the Gita*, vol. 13.

54. *Ibid.*, p. 98. See also "Doctrine of Passive Resistance," in *Bande Mataram*, 1: 127.

55. "Doctrine of Passive Resistance," in *Bande Mataram*, 1: 98. Within this context Aurobindo reflects on suffering as being an element intrinsic to passive resistance in contrast to the alternative position of retaliation through violence. He clearly values the role of suffering. See also "College Square Speech," in *Karmayogin*, 2: 114.

56. *Sri Aurobindo Mandir Annual*, no. 27 (August 15, 1968), p. 85.

57. *Talks with Sri Aurobindo* (Calcutta: Sri Aurobindo Pathamandir, 1966), p. 187.

58. "Doctrine of Passive Resistance," in *Bande Mataram*, pp. 101-4. See also "An Open Letter to My Countrymen," in *Karmayogin*, 2: 128. Though Aurobindo saw the tax boycott to be the strongest form of passive resistance, he felt that unlike political boycott it would be impractical, due to the legal reprisals it necessarily precipitates. See "Doctrine of Passive Resistance," in *Bande Mataram*, 1: 104-5, 120-21.

59. "Doctrine of Passive Resistance," *ibid.*, p. 106.

60. *Harmony of Virtue* 3: 363.

61. *Ibid.*

62. "Nivritti or Abstention" (1909), trans. Jugal Kishore Mukherji, *Sri Aurobindo Mandir Annual*, no. 27 (August 15, 1968), pp. 11-12, including translator's n1.

63. "An Open Letter to My Countrymen," in *Karmayogin*, 2: 125.

64. "Doctrine of Passive Resistance," in *Bande Mataram*, 1: 110-15.

65. "To My Countrymen," in *Karmayogin*, 2: 326. This article, published December 25, 1909, became the source of intense debate among the English in meetings of the House of Commons in 1910. See Das, *Sri Aurobindo*, pp. 140-61 and "An Open Letter to My Countrymen," in *Karmayogin, 2: 127-28.*

66. "Doctrine of Passive Resistance," in *Bande Mataram*, 1: 110; see pp. 110-14, where Aurobindo affirms the best response to opposition from within: social boycott or excommunication—a necessary element for an effective and strong front.

67. "The Awakening Soul of India," in *Karmayogin*, 2: 37.

68. "Our Hope" (1910), *Sri Aurobindo Mandir Annual*, no. 27 (August 15, 1968), pp. 23-24.

69. "Doctrine of Passive Resistance," in *Bande Mataram*, 1: 114.

70. *Ibid.*, p. 116. While the saint and the philanthropist exhibit an admirable love for others, Aurobindo feels that the masses of mankind do not—in fact, cannot—exhibit such selflessness. Consequently, it is unrealistic and unfair for anyone to make impossible demands on people to practice passive resistance under all circumstances. Passive resistance, though not an act of hate, "is an act of self-defence, of aggression for the sake of self-preservation" (*ibid.*, p. 125).

In this context, too, Aurobindo again approvingly alludes to the caste system, which sets a variety of ideals for a variety of types of people. There is one "for the saint, another for the man of action, a third for the trader, a fourth for the serf." Not to so distinguish is to confuse these separate duties and to destroy the society and the race.

71. *Ibid.*, p. 117. "Morality of Boycott," in *Bande Mataram*, 1: 126-27.

72. "Morality of Boycott," in *Bande Mataram*, 1: 127.

73. "To My Countrymen," in *Karmayogin*, 2: 326.

74. "The Ideal of the Karmayogin," in *Karmayogin*, 2: 19.

75. "More About Unity" (December 4, 1907), in *Bande Mataram*, 1: 622.

76. "The New Faith," in *Bande Mataram*, 1: 613.

77. In 1950 Aurobindo wrote with a vision of retrospect: "India is free and her freedom was necessary if the divine work was to be done." *On Himself*, 26: 172.

78. On freedom as a value and goal, see "The Nagpur Affair and True Unity" (October 23, 1907), in *Bande Mataram*, 1: 566-68. On the importance of unity, see for example, "The Work Before Us" (April 12, 1908), in *Bande Mataram*, 1: 847-49.

79. See as an example "Prison and Freedom," *Sri Aurobindo Mandir Annual*, no. 27 (August 15, 1968), pp. 157, 159.

80. *Ibid.*, p. 157.

81. *Ibid.*, p. 158. See also "Man—Slave or Free?" in *The Harmony of Virtue*,

3: 376-78, where Aurobindo claims that yoga asserts man's freedom from matter, giving him a means to express that freedom and thus reject the fallacies of materialistic doctrine.

82. "Prison and Freedom," *Sri Aurobindo Mandir Annual*, no. 27 (August 15, 1968), p. 158.

83. *Ibid.*, pp. 158-63.

84. "Karmayoga," in *Harmony of Virtue*, 3: 343-44. See also "Asceticism and Renunciation," *Sri Aurobindo Mandir Annual*, no. 26 (August 15, 1967), p. 61.

85. "The Three Purushas," in *Harmony of Virtue*, 3: 373.

86. *Ibid.*, pp. 372-73. In an article "Yoga and Hypnotism," in *Harmony of Virtue*, 3: 387, Aurobindo maintains that science would agree with him also and points to hypnotism as the "first real proof which Science has had of the power of action independent of volition." Contrary to popular misconception, the hypnotist does not substitute his will for that of the subject in sleep. Rather, the acitivities engaged in by the subject result from the volition of the subject but not in a spontaneous way; rather the subject's volition "is used as a slave by the operator working through the medium of suggestion." His point is to show the analogy between yoga and hypnotism with respect to volition: "The difference between Yoga and hypnotism is that what hypnotism does for a man through the agency of another and in the sleeping state, Yoga does for him by his own agency and in the waking state" (*ibid.*, p. 389).

87. In an article on "'Freewill' in Sri Aurobindo's Vision," K. D. Sethna comments that even when the individual acts as something involved in Prakriti, the act still "carries a touch of freedom with it; for that involvement, that enslavement, is freely made and there remains with us the power to withhold sanction to the current play of Nature in our members and to bring about a turn towards the Perfect, the Divine, the Un-enslaved" (in *The Vision and Work of Sri Aurobindo* [Pondicherry: Mother India, 1968], p. 95). Note the publisher's introductory comment to the book, which claims that Sri Aurobindo read and approved with enthusiasm the understanding Sethna exhibited in the essay.

88. *Harmony of Virtue*, 3: 379-82.

89. *Ibid.*, p. 380.

90. *Ibid.*, p. 381.

91. *Ibid.*, p. 382.

92. *Ibid.* It is evident from letters to his wife, Mrinalini, explaining his continued absence, that Aurobindo surrendered in this way so fully that he felt he had become a "puppet" of the Divine and was no longer his own master, no longer free; everything he did was done according to the command of the Divine. His letters were written to help Mrinalini understand and accept this and the life-style it imposed upon her. See "Letter" (1907), in *Sri Aurobindo Mandir Annual*, no. 26 (August 15, 1967), pp. 117-22, particularly p. 121.

93. "The Three Purushas," in *Harmony of Virtue*, 3: 373.

94. "Man—Slave or Free?" in *Harmony of Virtue*, 3: 375. In "Yoga and Hypnotism," in *Harmony of Virtue*, 3: 390, Aurobindo writes: "It is con-

ceivable . . . that the practice of Yoga by a great number of men and persistence might bring about profound changes in human psychology and, by stamping these changes into body and brain through heredity, evolve a superior race which would endure and by the law of the survival of the fittest eliminate the weaker kinds of humanity. Just as the rudimentary mind of the animal has been evolved into the fine instrument of the human being so the rudiments of higher force and faculty in the present race might evolve into the perfect *buddhi* of the Yogin.''

95. ''Man—Slave or Free?'' in *Harmony of Virtue*, 3: 376-77.

96. *Ibid.*, p. 377. In ''Yoga and Human Evolution,'' in *Harmony of Virtue*, 3: 357, Aurobindo acknowledges that this point sharply identifies the difference between the Western materialistic theories of human progress from the Indian theory: ''According to the scientific theory, the human being began as the animal, developed through the savage and consummated in the modern civilized man. The Indian theory is different. God created the world by developing the many out of the One and the material out of the spiritual.'' See also pp. 359-61.

97. ''Yoga and Human Evolution,'' in *Harmony of Virtue*, 3: 358.

98. *Ibid.*, p. 359.

99. *Ibid.*, p. 360; also p. 361.

100. ''Yoga and Hypnotism,'' in *Harmony of Virtue*, 3: 392.

101. ''The Ideal of the Karmayogin,'' in *Karmayogin*, 2: 18, also p. 21. ''Karmayoga,'' in *Harmony of Virtue*, 3: 343. See also K. Singh, *Prophet*, p. 81.

102. *Sri Aurobindo Mandir Annual*, no. 27 (August 15, 1968), pp. 120-73.

103. *Karmayogin*, 2: 1-10.

104. *Ibid.*, p. 8.

105. *Ibid.*, p. 4.

106. ''The Present Situation'' (1908), in *Bande Mataram*, 1: 665. (Italics mine.)

107. ''Ideals Face to Face'' (1908), in *Bande Mataram*, 1: 902.

4

The Meaning of Spiritual Liberation

> I came to Pondicherry in order to have freedom and tranquillity for a
> fixed object having nothing to do with present politics—in which I
> have taken no direct part since my coming here, though what I could
> do for the country in my own way I have constantly done,—and until it
> is accomplished, it is not possible for me to resume any kind of public
> activity.[1]

Divine life for humanity was the "fixed object" that moved Aurobindo to
leave the active world of politics and revolution for the retired world of
contemplation at Pondicherry.

To his friends and critics, Aurobindo's life in Pondicherry came as a
surprise; at best it was a disappointment, at worst an escape. Yet Aurobindo claimed that his retirement was not prompted by any lack of
concern for the success of the political hopes of India; rather, he felt a
personal "command from above" and experienced a "call to go to
Pondicherry"[2] as a means of bringing about a larger liberation, which
would affect not only India but all the world. From Pondicherry, Aurobindo wrote in 1920 that he was certain that India would one day
achieve political freedom, but that what concerned him most was what
India would do with its freedom.[3]

Later that year, in another letter, Aurobindo explored his feelings once
again on the subject of leaving politics:

> Why have I left politics? Because the politics of the country is not a

genuine thing belonging to India. It is an importation from Europe and an imitation. At one time there was a need for it. We also have done politics of the European kind. If we had not done it, the country would not have risen and we too would not have gained experience and attained full development. There is still some need of it, not so much in Bengal as in the other provinces of India. But the time has come to extend no longer the shadow but seize on the reality. We must get to the true soul of India and in its image fashion all works.[4]

Again in 1932 he spoke to this question:

I did not leave politics because I felt I could do nothing more there; such an idea was very far from me. I came away because I did not want anything to interfere with my Yoga and because I got a very distinct *ādeśa* in the matter. I have cut connection entirely with politics, but before I did so I knew from within that the work I had begun there was destined to be carried forward, on lines I had foreseen, by others, and that the ultimate triumph of the movement I had initiated was sure without my personal action or presence. There was not the least motive of despair or sense of futility behind my withdrawal.[5]

Addressing himself to the question of freedom in the early days of his Pondicherry period,[6] Aurobindo observes that we always tend to think in contradictions or oppositions and that one of the most dominant examples is the tension between the perception that we are determined and the perception that we are free. So much in our lives is determined by our environment, educational background, family heredity, and cultural up-bringing, and we readily acknowledge and admit these to be powerful determinants. Yet we insist that however burdened we are with deter-minisms of this sort and variety, we are nonetheless possessors of some degree of freedom; with effort we can change our environment, redirect the influences of our upbringing, heredity, and cultural expectations.[7]

Aurobindo begins to unravel this dilemma by affirming that if we in fact do have a will that is to some degree free, such a claim makes sense "only if there is a soul or self which is not a creation, but a master of Nature, not a formation of the stream of universal energy, but itself the former and creator of its own Karma."[8] Rejecting the ancient Buddhist and the modern materialist oppositions on the basis that they perpetuate a bifurcated handling of the problem (cosmic compulsion on the one hand, over against a spiritual freedom or release that negates worldly existence on the other hand), Aurobindo proceeds to sketch a view that synthesizes the experience of determinism and freedom.

He notes that the impression we have of freedom is something that relates intimately to our experience of mind. We do not speak of the world of matter as a world marked by freedom. Things occur in process, according to discoverable patterns we call "laws," but we sense no conscious action of intelligence as we do in human behavior. If matter were all we observed, we could rest content with a theory of determinism. But we see more than mechanical movements; we see also mental movements, become aware of possibilities and choice, and continue to be aware of a variety of "'may-be's" and "'might-have-been's.'"[9]

These movements of the mind can go further; the mind "can conceive of an infinite possibility behind the self-limitations of actual existence . . . . of a free and infinite Will . . . [which] determines Karma." And so Aurobindo concludes,

Apparent Necessity is the child of the Spirit's free self-determination. What affects us as Necessity, is a Will which works in sequence and not a blind Force driven by its own mechanism.[10]

Yet he admits the nonnecessity of accepting this explanation, and he nods to alternative interpretations that hold for a nothingness behind necessity, or a spiritual reality predestining things, or a spiritual reality marked by absolute freedom allowing other beings some (though limited) degree of participation in that freedom.

Aurobindo resolves the problem of determinism and freedom in this way: The soul of man is a power of the self-existence which manifests the universe and not the creature and slave of a mechanical Nature; and it is only the natural instruments of his being, it is mind, life and body and their functions and members which are helpless apparatus and gear of the machinery.[11]

While these "gear" are subject to karma, "the real man within is not its subject."[12]

On the contrary, karma becomes one's instrument in the evolution to a divine and cosmic personality. Although the individual may indeed be capable of a release, a liberation into the infinite with its simultaneous cessation of action, mind, and personality, this is not the whole of spiritual freedom or liberation. For a person is more than an outward individual being; in the inner and true self one is an individual spiritual being and hence is capable of participating in the full freedom of the spirit.

In the mental existence this freedom is relative, for the individual lives in outward ignorance and is subject to its limitations. Until one discovers the "real centre," the soul, which when finally developed, "can come forward and control the nature,"[13] the person remains the prime target for rule by the surface self. The individual continues to be vulnerable to the physical body and its narrow concern for bodily wants; or one will be governed by the vital self with its preoccupation for self-affirmation, ambition, and ego-claims; finally, the person might be ruled by the mental self subordinating other wants to mental ideas and ideals. And even though mind has greater control than the vital or physical levels, it cannot fully master those inclinations which are powerful in their resistance to integration with the whole being and nature.[14]

Yet a person is capable of glimpsing "at least a potential absolute freedom behind it [the relative freedom]."[15] Sometimes we confuse these two and thus live in the conviction that we are already fully free. Eventually we can become so if we move toward, surrender to, and enter supramental existence. But only in that state above the mental is full freedom possible. Until then, our relative freedom expresses itself by way of assent and agreement, allowing us to be moved by the laws of nature, to discover and acquiesce to karma in obedience. We can also give expression to this relative freedom by refusing to assent, thus effecting a condition in which karma eventually loses power. Whichever the response, the freedom is relative and for Aurobindo "not well distinguishable from a lightened bondage."[16]

The freedom that comes with growth into the Spirit is also at first a passive power, which takes expression in assent. But here the assent is given not to the mechanical movements of nature (as in the relative freedom described above) but to the will of the Spirit, which in turn showers the mind with light and with knowledge about the nature of divine workings. From this level of freedom we can move to a fuller participation and power in which "as the son of God"[17] we rise beyond the levels of the mind and enter the realm of supermind, where karma itself becomes evident as part of the rhythm of freedom.[18] The intrinsically ambiguous and even paradoxical nature of freedom (Aurobindo would not say contradictory, given his discussion as just detailed) continued to haunt Aurobindo as his days at Pondicherry continued.

Writing on this topic during World War I, he distinguishes freedom seen from the temporal point of view from freedom considered from an inward, more spiritual point of view. *War and Self-Determination* contains a description of what liberty is not.

> when we start from the natural and temporal life, what we practically come to mean by liberty is a convenient elbow-room for our natural energies to satisfy themselves without being too much impinged upon by the self-assertiveness of others. And that is a difficult problem to solve, because the liberty of one, immediately it begins to act, knocks up fatally against the liberty of another; the free running of many in the same field means a free chaos of collisions.[19]

Yet, in spite of this search for liberty, which often expresses itself in mere self-interest and excessive self-concern, he is haunted by the realization that "liberty in one shape or another ranks among the most ancient and certainly among the most difficult aspirations of our race." Liberty is grounded in a "radical instinct" of our being and yet, while it remains our "eternal good" and "condition of perfection,"[20] it has failed to take shape in temporal existence. In this context of conjecture about the "why" of such failure, Aurobindo discloses his view of what genuine liberty really is:

> true freedom is only possible if we live in the infinite, live, as the Vedanta bids us, in and from our self-existent being....This great indefinable thing, liberty, is in its highest and ultimate sense a state of being; it is self living in itself and determining by its own energy what it shall be inwardly, and, eventually, by the growth of a divine spiritual power within determining too what it shall make of its external circumstances and environment; that is the largest and freest sense of self-determination.[21]

Later in the same context, Aurobindo writes that the principle of self-determination really means that in everyone—man, woman, child—there is discoverable "a self, a being, which has the right to grow in its own way, to find itself, to make its life a full and a satisfied instrument and image of its being."[22] Although he admits the ease with which this inclination can degenerate into egoistic self-satisfaction, he maintains that as a principle it is to prevail; everything else is a question of means.

Native to human life is a yearning for the opportunity to grow, to achieve, to exceed and thereby fulfill oneself, continually to evolve to higher and higher levels of consciousness. In its largest meaning the process of spiritual evolution, which ultimately ushers in complete liberation, transforms soul, mind, heart, and action into the unity of the cosmic and transcendent Divine Reality.[23]

This transformation occurs gradually and in three distinct stages. First there is a psychic change, during which the spirit becomes discernible as distinct from mind and the body processes; second, there is the spiritual change, which takes place as a higher light, knowledge, and power descend into and permeate the whole being; a third change, referred to by Aurobindo as "the supramental transmutation," is the ascent into supermind, with the consequent descent of the supramental consciousness transforming one's entire being and nature (19:891, 912).

The ascent is the movement of the consciousness to higher planes of consciousness; the descent is the movement of these higher planes into earth-consciousness, driving out ignorance and transforming nature. Of these higher planes (higher, illumined, intuitive mind, and overmind, as well as supermind), supermind alone is free from the vulnerable position of losing its own power by being modified, diluted, or diminished. Supermind alone is able finally to effect the being's liberation and fulfillment. In Aurobindo's words, "As the psychic change has to call in the spiritual to complete it, so the first spiritual change has to call in the supramental transformation to complete it" (19:917-18).

Yet, because of Aurobindo's cosmic consciousness and concern, a personal transformation is not an end in itself. Individual transformation gains "permanent and cosmic significance" only when the transformed being becomes "a centre and a sign for the establishment of the supramental Consciousness-Force as an overtly operative power in the terrestrial workings of Nature . . ." (19:962). Essential to the personal transformation is its power to signify for others the immanence of the supramental.

Since the process of transformation intimately touches on the goal of that process, it seems pertinent now to press for meaning regarding the goal to which this transformation leads before asking about the means by which it can happen.

The Goal of Spiritual Freedom:
Supramental Transformation

The goal of the liberating, transforming process of evolution is the establishment of the supramental consciousness-force that is expressed in the appearance of the Gnostic Being. It must be admitted at the outset that it is difficult if not impossible to describe the gnostic being with any accuracy, for it is supramental in nature. Consequently, there is a serious epistemological problem rooted in the fact that Aurobindo's source of knowledge about the gnostic being is an "innate spiritual vision" (19:965) and not a mental idea communicable on the basis of assumed analogous experience. Aurobindo was keenly conscious of this epistemological gap.

A mental description of supramental nature could only express itself either in phrases which are too abstract or in mental figures which might turn it into something quite different from its reality. It would not seem to be possible, therefore, for the mind to anticipate or indicate what a supramental being shall be or how he shall act; for here mental ideas and formulations cannot decide anything or arrive at any precise definition or determination, because they are not near enough to the law and self-vision of supramental nature. (19:966)

But the discussion is not to be aborted at this point, as is evident from Aurobindo's continuation of the passage:

At the same time certain deductions can be made from the very fact of this difference of nature which might be valid at least for a general description of the passage from Overmind to Supermind or might vaguely construct for us an idea of the first status of the evolutionary supramental existence. (19:966)

A helpful analogy employed early in his discussion of the gnostic being is this: as there has been a mental consciousness and power operative on earth, shaping a race of mental beings and assuming into itself all earthly nature ripe for change, so there will now be present a gnostic consciousness and power able to shape a race of gnostic beings and assume whatever earthly nature is ready for this next transformation (19:967).

This transformation will be marked by the two-fold movement of ascent from below and descent from above, issuing in the transformation of inconscience to superconscience, darkness to light, ignorance to truth, mental being to the gnostic consciousness and nature (19:967-68).

A series of images captures more concretely the total impact of this change: the principle of "harmony" would become more dominant than discord, strife, and struggle; an interplay of "intuition," "sympathy," and "understanding" would be present in human life, enabling a "clearer sense" of the truth of things and a more "enlightened dealing" with the problems of existence (19:969). Above all, the presence of supermind would be felt in its "unitarian," "integralising," and "harmonic" trend while respecting the diversity of manifestation possible to the gnostic consciousness (19:970). But to delve into the nature of the gnostic being fully, Aurobindo maintains, would demand the insight of supermind alone. From the point of view of mental perception, only abstract outlines such as this are possible (19:971).

In relation to spirituality, the ultimate value and foundation of Aurobindo's system, the gnostic being is the perfection and fulfillment, "the consummation" of the "spiritual man"; "his whole way of being, thinking, living, acting would be governed by the power of a vast universal spirituality" (19:971-72).

The "spiritual man" of ethically or mystically oriented religious world views is not the same as the "gnostic being" of Aurobindo. It seems clear from his perspective that, while the gnostic being is the consummation of the spiritual person, he or she is more than the spiritual person in that the gnostic being does not turn away from a world that is seen to be incapable of change, nor attempt to act on it while maintaining a sanctuary within, distant from that world. Rather, the gnostic individual experiences a true integration between the inner life and the outer life, for at that stage all antinomy between the self and the world is "cured and exceeded."[24]

A new relationship is established between the spirit and the body and now, with the gnostic transformation, there is possible

> a free acceptance of the whole of material Nature in place of a rejection; the drawing back from her, the refusal of all identification or acceptance, which is the first normal necessity of the spiritual consciousness for its liberation, is no longer imperative.[25]

In a word, the "spiritual man" is characterized by a liberation of the soul from the limitations of the body, from ignorance to awareness and consequent peace, calm, and silence in face of the discovery of the eternal. The gnostic being, however, goes beyond this spiritual liberation to participation in the fully experienced bliss of the eternal (19:990). He or she shares the divine nature (19:994).

> The gnostic life will exist and act for the Divine in itself and in the world, for the Divine in all; the increasing possession of the individual being and the world by the Divine Presence, Light, Power, Love, Delight. Beauty will be the sense of life to the gnostic being. (19:984)

The relationship between the spiritual person and the gnostic being, then, is this: an inner life of the spirit must be developed before divine living of the gnostic being becomes possible (19:984-85). And because the spiritual quest for perfection ordinarily stops with individual liberation, it is insufficient for an evolutionary perspective such as Aurobindo describes. For him spiritual liberation must open beyond itself to change existence in the surrounding environment, to change and perfect nature and all life, resulting in the appearance of a new order of beings and a new life that is divine (19:1020).

In this gnostic awareness, the beings would also experience a new freedom, a "transcendent freedom" in which they would live and act. Their joy would be complete; they would sense an identity with the cosmos and identify with everything in the universe. At this point Aurobindo's language heightens in paradoxical allusions; gnostic beings would be in and of the world while transcendent to the world; they would be both universal and individual (19:972).

Aurobindo admits the inadequacy of mental perceptions to convey the full flavor of the gnostic experience. Perhaps most pointed and most honest is his comment that all the characteristics and qualities of the being would be perfected and integrated "in some kind of comprehensive largeness" (19:973). It is admittedly impossible for Aurobindo to verbalize adequately what he claims is essentially a transverbal, transmental, transnatural mode of being.

Also inadequate are ethical categories of good and evil to describe this perfection of gnostic existence. The supramental being has no need to be concerned with the good of others, striving to express empathy and compassion. Such a manner of being will be "intimate to his self-fulfilment, the fulfilment of the One in all, and there will be no contradiction or strife between his own good and the good of others . . ." (19:976).

Ethical decisions are dissolved in the establishment of the gnostic existence. Evil has given way to good, ignorance to knowledge, conflict to harmony, divisiveness to unity. Although the gnostic being exercises "control" and "the power of instrumentation" (19:980) on the rest of the world and nature, this power is by definition creative, filling, enriching, perfecting, completing; it brings life's quest for growth, satisfaction, possession, love, beauty, and the like to the highest expression possible. As a power of the gnostic being it cannot act destructively, narrowly, ambitiously (19:984); all conflict, all problems are eliminated (19:996, 999).

And so, according to Aurobindo, the ethical dimension of life is transcended. Just as subhuman life is infra-ethical in nature, so the suprahuman (gnostic) level of existence is supra-ethical in nature. The ethical realm is a necessary but temporary phase in the evolution; it is relevant only to the ego-centered consciousness at a certain stage. Eventually, laws become unnecessary because struggle and conflict are overcome in unity with the divine. At most "there is the law and self-order of the liberty of the Spirit, there can be no imposed or constructed law of conduct, dharma. All becomes a self-flow of spiritual self-nature . . . ."[26] Because the gnostic being participates in the nature of the divine, the liberty or freedom of spirit becomes identical with "an entire obedience of his nature" to the will of the divine.[27]

Clearly then, when Aurobindo describes the supramental gnostic being, his language is severely handicapped by historically conditioned connotations; an ethical language of paradox continues to emerge. In gnostic existence laws are transcended, yet a single law remains: the obedience to "self-truth and the total truth of Being." Furthermore, the freedom to choose the false and the untrue is likewise transcended, yet freedom still characterizes gnostic existence: "his freedom is a freedom of light, not of darkness" (19:1003). The foundation on which this gnostic freedom rests is the unity of the divine acting through the being and exhibiting the unity of the gnostic will with the will of the eternal (19:1006). When this happens, divine life has come to earth and one has achieved his highest possibilities and calling; he has begun to live fully, which means for Aurobindo to live wholly conscious of being, to live in possession of one's own force of being or will, to live in full delight, and to *be*, both universally and transcendentally (19:1023-25). As this divine life begins to take hold in more and more people, there will gradually be established a new unity, mutuality, and harmony of all (19:1035).

In sum, spiritual freedom or liberation carries more than a single meaning for Aurobindo. Spiritual liberation refers to the liberation of the spirit or self of one who seeks to discover the life within; the soul is liberated or freed as it were from the ignorance and boundaries of sheer bodily existence. Beyond this level of freedom or liberation, attained by the evolution of the spiritual being, there is a "transcendent freedom" (19:972) or an "infinite freedom" (19:1000) that characterizes the gnostic stage of the individual seeking completion.

From this consideration, freedom is to be recognized as both means and end, both process and purpose. As means and process, spiritual freedom or liberation refers to the release of the inner self (soul, spirit), formerly unrecognized in the busyness of bodily concerns and behavior. As end and purpose of life, spiritual freedom or liberation refers to the "dynamis of the gnostic Supernature" as an "entire freedom of the Spirit, an entire self-existent order self-creating, self-effectuating, self-secure in its own natural and inevitable movement'' (19:998). At the gnostic stage, freedom becomes synonymous with total obedience to the divine.[28]

Each of these delineations of freedom in the spiritual sphere marks each of the two phases of evolution: evolution in the ignorance that is marked by pain as well as joy, frustrations as well as fulfillments; and evolution in the knowledge that is the completion of the evolutionary process and characterized by a discovery of the spirit and revelation of the divine, which is unfolded in the discovery of the self and which transforms the being fully, bringing it to supramental, supranatural divine life.[29]

The significant theme to be noted at this point is the fact that spiritual freedom in either meaning is attainable only if one works to bring this about. And this raises the question: by what means can spiritual freedom be attained?

Means to Spiritual Freedom

By what means is a person able to enter into this freedom? By going inward to find the self. ''By living within and from within''[30] one will discover the self and the different parts and planes of the being. Too often people have only a surface view of themselves, identifying every part of themselves with the experience of the mind, since it is through the mind that they know or feel. But yoga is based on the conviction that we can and should become conscious of our complexity and learn to discern the variety of forces moving us.[31]

Aurobindo distinguishes two chief planes, the surface self and the real self. The surface self is constituted by the physical (the body and its functions), the vital (emotion, desire, feeling), and the mental (the mind and its functions). However, the real (inner) self is also constituted by these three dimensions, analogous to and ''behind'' the surface components. There are, in other words, an ''inner physical,'' an ''inner vital,'' and an ''inner mind,'' which enable the individual to achieve contact with the liberating and universal truth of all selves and all things.[32]

One of the first steps in the practice of yoga, and one of the first fruits emerging from this turning within, is the discovery of these different dimensions of the self as surface and inner through a separation of one from the other. What is experienced is a separation of the being from thought, from life movements such as desire and sensation, and from body sense. These separations provide the clarity needed for the individual yogi to freshly discern himself in his deepest self as spirit: "spirit in mind . . . spirit supporting life . . . spirit ensouling Matter." [33]

The point of contact between the surface and inner selves with the higher levels of consciousness is the psychic level, which is seen as an opening allowing the individual to ascend to higher levels of consciousness and allowing the supreme consciousness a point of entry in order that it may descend and transform the surface self. In its fullest meaning the psychic is not only a point of contact but a spark and presence of the divine within. [34]

Though a difficult task for the normal human consciousness, this is the only way for one to find oneself. [35] The finding occurs in the reuniting of the divine and all of nature in a fully liberated, perfected human life. [36]

From this point of view, yoga is a microcosmic and personal, condensed version of the cosmic process of evolution: it also (like evolution) is a method by which the spirit is liberated. As Aurobindo's understanding of evolution explains the relationships among the transcendental, the universal, and the individual, so too, yoga rests upon the co-presence of these three (God, nature, and the human soul), and their ultimate union in the supramental divine life on earth.

Many yogas have been developed in the attempt to create a contact between the divine and the human consciousness. Hathayoga focuses on the physical or gross body as its means of perfection; Rajayoga selects the mental being or subtle-body for its pathway; Karmayoga centers on works, Bhakti Yoga on the heart, Jnana Yoga on the intellect as each seeks to enable entry into the spiritual life. [37] What all these methods have in common is the assumption that in the end "all power is soul-power." [38] And all of them seek liberation as the means to achieve soul-power, whether that be liberation from the necessities of physical nature (hathayoga), from subjection to sensation, emotion, enjoyment (rajayoga), or from ordinary and external preoccupations prompted by intellect, heart, or will (jnanayoga, bhaktiyoga, karmayoga). The *liberation from* is always a *liberation to*: from limitation to perfection, from the confines of material existence to unity with the infinite divine existence.

In light of these forms of yoga, Aurobindo proposes the possibility of designing a new yoga form. Whereas the ordinary yogic viewpoint involves "rejection of the lower and escape into the higher," Aurobindo's yoga involves "transformation of the lower and its elevation to the higher."[39] Aurobindo's vision of the Integral Yoga implies the attempt to enter into contact with the divine, but it also refers to the full and difficult process by the divine in preparing the entire lower nature that it may become the higher nature, and the eventual transformation itself together with the new role of this transformed humanity as a divine center in the world.[40]

One's conversion from concern for the without to a newly discovered concern for the within surfaces a new consciousness of the inner parts of one's nature. Following this conversion a series of conversions occur whereby there is a movement of ascent toward the higher planes of being, which in turn brings on a movement of descent touching and converting the lower planes. This is the process in which "one psychicises the whole lower nature so as to make it ready for the divine change."[41] The stages of the ascent raise one to ever higher levels of consciousness: beyond intellect to illumined mind, beyond this to a still higher intuitive consciousness, on again to the heights of overmind, and finally, from the levels of overmind consciousness to the supramental level of consciousness where one is beyond the Ignorance.[42]

As an integral yoga this method is intended to usher in an integral liberation that transforms as well as frees. Furthermore, it is a liberation not confined to the individual but extending to include the liberation of others and all humanity. "The perfect utility of our perfection is, having realised in ourselves the divine symbol, to reproduce, multiply and ultimately universalise it in others."[43]

In constructing this yoga that attempts to embrace all of life rather than reject or deny it, Aurobindo finds himself in the position of pathfinder far more than pilgrim: hewing a new road rather than following one that has been well worn.[44] Consequently this newly emerging yoga cannot be bound by any written or traditional principles. Though not closed to the wisdom of such principles, the new yoga is intended to honor a complete openness to that Veda secret in the heart of each person. For the Infinite is perceived not only as transcendent truth to be sought for, but as the immanent infinite to be unfolded in human life.[45]

It is the very condition of this yoga to be open to inner experience and to suggest only the broadest of general principles; these are not intended to be a fixed and rigid system but to be statements of directions intended to guide. They are the signposts the pathfinder leaves as his contribution to later pioneers.[46]

Disciplined effort is another condition necessary to this yoga. But the achievement of human effort can be deceptive. In the egoism before enlightenment or realization, one tends to think that he is free and claims to effect numerous movements by virtue of personal will, wisdom, or force. But in reality, what is felt as freedom is in fact a

> pitiable subjection to a thousand suggestions, impulsions, forces which we have made extraneous to our little person. Our ego, boasting of freedom, is at every moment, the slave, toy and puppet of countless beings, powers, forces, influences in universal Nature.[47]

Perfect freedom or liberation comes only in surrender to that which transcends it.[48] It is crucial for the sadhak to discern the movement of divine grace and gradually to recognize that it is always "the higher Power that acts."[49]

While the place of the guide or guru as helper and source of insight is a third condition of yoga, Aurobindo places the primary (though not exclusive) focus on an "inner Guide . . . secret within us."[50] This is the teacher, who discloses the love, freedom, bliss, and power that are sought, and who transforms the lower existence into the higher.

Finally, the place of time and a realistic and respectful acceptance of it by the yogi are a key condition for entry into yoga. This demands patience toward the slow and natural rhythm of growth as it occurs in successive stages. And it demands the repeated exercise of "free choice"[51] to inhibit interference from the lower nature as the individual seeks contact with and realization of the higher nature. Fulfillment comes slowly.[52]

Always the emphasis in Aurobindo's integral yoga is the importance of listening to "the within". The Veda within one's heart is the chief source of yogic knowledge; the personal and inner surrender to the transcendent power is the key disposition to be encouraged, and it is the inner guide or internal guru who is to be followed above all others. The thrust toward the immanent is underscored again and again:

> The Divine that we adore is not only a remote extracosmic Reality, but a half-veiled Manifestation present and near to us here in the universe. Life is the field of a divine manifestation not yet complete: here, in life, on earth, in the body . . .we have to unveil the God-head.[53]

That unveiling process is fostered and accelerated by one's ever-deepening entry into the life of work, knowledge, and love, the contexts by which a person can make contact with the divine.

For those whose inclinations are primarily oriented to the world of work and the exercise of will, karmayoga is an available method for achieving freedom in the spirit.[54] For those inclined to the knowledge that comes from study and meditation, the way of knowledge provides an entry, and for those whose movement is largely one of devotion, the path of love invites them in its way. Each path one chooses leads to the others and eventually the paths of works, of knowledge, and of love are experienced simultaneously rather than successively.

Common to each path, however, are the means of concentration and renunciation by which the hoped-for object of liberation and eventual transformation can be attained. Although there are various intensities of concentration,[55] each moves the individual into an unwavering and undistracted pursuit of a single topic of thought issuing in the cessation of thought itself in a state of pure and absorbed contemplation where the mind is altogether still. Quiet, silence, and peaceful stillness provide an atmosphere conducive to the individual's coming into conscious contact with the psychic plane.

> When there is a complete silence in the being, either a stillness of the whole being or a stillness behind unaffected by surface movements, then we can become aware of a Self, a spiritual substance of our being,

an existence exceeding even the soul-individuality, spreading itself into universality, surpassing all dependence on any natural form or action, extending itself upward into a transcendence of which the limits are not visible. It is these liberations of the spiritual part in us which are the decisive steps of the spiritual evolution in Nature.[56]

Aurobindo's central point in this analysis is the recognition that there is a distinction between spiritual consciousness and mental consciousness, between our deep spiritual being and our surface mental personality.[57]

The evolution of the mental and the spiritual is a double evolution touching the outward nature and the inner being. And though the discovery of the mental level cannot be confused with the spiritual, it must be allowed and encouraged to evolve to its fullest possibilities. For only then will it be possible for there to be the disclosure of the intuitive mind, of overmind and supermind and the passage to these higher instruments of the Spirit.[58] Eventually this becomes a knowledge of the divine that is not something that is known, but something rather that takes possession of the consciousness in all its parts and planes.[59]

Renunciation as a means to yogic completion is particularly pertinent to uncovering further the theme of freedom. Aurobindo reminds us that a long-favored tradition of many religious teachings holds that renunciation is not only a discipline but also an end, completed in the renunciation of life itself and earthly existence. But for the sadhaka of the integral yoga, renunciation is solely an instrument and never an object. Furthermore it is not the only nor even the central instrument, since the whole point of integral yoga is "the fulfilment of the Divine in the human being."[60]

It is true, Aurobindo continues, that we cannot be attached to life in the world and must therefore be capable of renunciation. But it is just as true that "neither shall we have any attachment to the escape from the world, to salvation, to the great self-annihilation; if that attachment exists, that also we must renounce and renounce it utterly."[61] The renunciation encouraged in integral yoga is the inward renunciation of desire, of self-will, of egoism—those ties which bind one to the lower nature, thereby retarding an openness to the higher nature.[62] Even the desire for liberation itself must be abandoned in order for one to be truly free.[63]

The positive thrust to be released by the spirit and discipline of renunciation is spiritual freedom itself. In the integral yoga this freedom is possible only through subjection of oneself to the higher being, self-surrender in silence and passivity. This paradoxically promotes entry into the dynamic activity of oneness with the eternal transcendent and cosmic Brahman.[64]

A person's sense of free will, according to Aurobindo, is largely an illusory sense because it is, in fact, nature that determines one's actions and life. In a sense human free will is real, but only in a relative way. We have the sense of choosing, yet fail to be aware of the force behind our will determining the choices we think we are making. If we continue in this line of thinking we become a victim of our "shackled so-called free will,"[65] whereas if we enter the route of yoga we will come to realize that the only absolutely free will in the world is the one divine will, and that our real freedom consists in living in the unifying reality of the eternal and divine will.[66]

To be in touch with this divine will is not, for Aurobindo, to be in touch with some "alien Power or Presence; it is intimate to us and we ourselves are part of it: for it is our own highest Self that possesses and supports it."[67] It must be remembered that this yoga of integral perfection is based on an image of man that views him as a "divine spiritual being involved in mind, life and body."[68]

The growth process accelerated by the discipline of yoga is a gradual one in which the soul increases in its power over the nature, enabling the individual to break through the limitations of his binding imperfections. In its rise on the scale of consciousness and existence, the soul becomes aware of its free will and control. Complete mastery emerges "when the Divine within . . . acts as the omnipotent master of the nature. For the Divine is our highest Self and the Self of all Nature, the eternal and universal Purusha."[69]

Consequently one's allegiance begins to shift as the sadhaka realizes that one is to be free in the spirit and subject only to the supreme truth. He no longer considers existing mental and moral laws as binding. A new divine law beckons his allegiance and loyalty. He has entered the transcendent, the transethical.[70] The fundamental trait of the liberated life is the spontaneous working of Prakriti, not through or for the ego, but at the movement of and for the happiness of the Supreme Purusha.[71]

Another significant trait of this liberated, perfected life is its communal—and not only individual—nature. There is a new sense of unity, an intense oneness permeating all being. The divisiveness that characterizes mental existence is now replaced with love, justice, and equality, which flow spontaneously without effort, without struggle, without quarrel.[72] This communal quality of liberation indicates Aurobindo's dissatisfaction with a yoga that remains content with an inner experience alone. His yoga is deliberately designed as a movement without as well as a movement within. The discovery of "the within" is followed by its transformation and outward expression, in a process in which the divine within touches and transforms that which is without.[73]

The direction of the integral yoga of self-perfection that Aurobindo describes has, then, three objects: first, the liberation of the individual and spiritual union with the divine; second, free enjoyment of the cosmic oneness of the divine; and third, the effecting of the divine oneness with all beings by an identification and participation in the spiritual purpose of the divine in humankind. The individual yoga moves from its separateness to the collective yoga and becomes an instrument of the divine in humanity.[74]

Thus the yoga of knowledge, love, and works is expanded into a yoga of spiritual and gnostic self-perfection, whereby the mental being enlarges and extends itself into union with the divine before the divine fulfills and completes the individual soul. This two-fold movement in the growth process is the primary aim of this yoga and is the reason Aurobindo labels it "integral": not only does it facilitate union with the divine but facilitates "complete enjoyment and possession of the whole divine and spiritual nature; and it is a complete lifting of the whole nature of man into its power of a divine and spiritual existence."[75] Given Aurobindo's insistence on the integral quality of his yoga of self-perfection, we need now ask how this yoga is integral to, or at least in some way related to, the theme of political freedom during the Pondicherry period. Furthermore, how did Aurobindo live this relationship as well as conceptualize it?

The Relationship between Political Freedom and Spiritual Freedom

As indicated in chapter 1 of this study, Aurobindo said that he was committed to using the spiritual power released in yoga in order to bring about the political liberation of his country. Upon his release from jail, the certitude he enjoyed that the work he had begun would be carried on without him enabled Aurobindo to express his inclination to devote himself totally to spiritual rather than political avenues of work.

In September 1935, Aurobindo was asked by a disciple, Nirodbaran, whether he felt convinced that India would be free; Nirodbaran pleaded with Aurobindo to effect her independence with his spiritual power. Aurobindo's response as recorded was:

> Have I not told you that the independence is all arranged for and will evolve itself all right. Then what's the use of my bothering about that any longer? It's what she will do with her independence that is not arranged for—and it is that about which I have to bother.[76]

Among other concerns, he was "bothered" by the war and wrote in 1944 that his spiritual force was being applied for the right development of the war and the change in the world at large.[77] Specifically, he claimed to have had an effective impact on other historical movements in Spain, Ireland, Turkey, and the Russian Revolution.[78] His intervention during World War II in support of the Cripps offer is one of the rare moments during his Pondicherry period when he made a public plea for the position he preferred. His position, however, was an unpopular one. Congress had little sympathy for Britain and still less loyalty, and as a consequence, Aurobindo's first public pronouncement since 1926 was not accepted as a norm for action. Sensing his ineffectiveness in the political forum he concentrated ever more fully in the spiritual forum.[79]

In his Independence Day Declaration, August 15, 1947, Aurobindo spoke to the issue of political and spiritual liberation in disclosing once again his conviction that India as a free nation was capable of playing a large and leading part in the future of humanity, politically, socially, culturally, and spiritually.[80]

The fact that August 15 is also Aurobindo's birth date suggested to him that this was not simply chance, but was divine affirmation indicating that Aurobindo's once-held dreams were now becoming historical realities. His first dream had been a revolutionary movement designed to bring about a free and united India. That day the freedom had become fact. Because of the partition separating Hindus and Muslims, however, unity remained hope rather than reality. Aurobindo spoke strongly that this division should be a temporary expedient at most and not a lasting resolution.[81]

His second dream concerned the resurgence and freedom of the Asian peoples to participate significantly in the progress of civilization. A third dream pointed to a world union that would invoke a brighter and better world for all people. Aurobindo considered such a unification, though clearly incomplete, to be definitely in process. Fourth, he dreamed that India would bring its gift of spirituality to the entire world, and he saw that movement growing. His final dream envisioned a new step in the evolutionary process, whereby people would rise to a greater and fuller consciousness and embark upon solving the problems that perplex them. Though still a personal hope, Aurobindo felt this ideal to be something shared by other forward-looking persons and therefore capable of communal achievement, even though he knew that the way would be a slow and difficult one.

In a word, Aurobindo did not perceive India's freedom as political conquest, or national victory, or the gaining of international prestige nearly as much as it signified the divine will and determination. India's freedom, though a clear and unambiguous value for Aurobindo, is always seen as an instrument for a greater freedom. Eight months before his death, he wrote that "[India's] freedom was necessary if the divine work was to be done."[82]

Summary

We have seen that Aurobindo's appreciation of political freedom was set against a larger horizon of a freedom that he called inner freedom or spiritual freedom or freedom of the spirit. It was to spend his time and energy on this larger sense of freedom or liberation that prompted Aurobindo to live at Pondicherry and to limit his participation in the public forum almost solely to his writings, particularly those published in *Arya*.

In analyzing the problem of freedom versus determinism, Aurobindo submits to neither as having an exclusive hold on the truth, but includes both in a desire to work out a synthetic interpretation that absorbs the truthfulness of each. He articulates such a synthesis in his concept of spirit, which is experienced as a determining force to those limited by ignorance, but is experienced as a freeing force to those who have entered the realms of higher consciousness.

The highest sphere of consciousness, supermind, is the goal to which people are called and it is achieved only after a gradual transforming process that brings about three decisive changes in the life of the individual: the psychic transformation, the spiritual transformation, and the final supramental transformation.

The supramental transformed being, also known as the gnostic being, is characterized by knowledge, bliss, power, freedom; he is beyond conflict, consequently beyond ethical struggle and decision-making. He is the fulfillment of the traditional "spiritual man," differing from this traditional image in that he does not eschew his body but accepts it anew and experiences it as a sign and center of divine presence.

Spiritual freedom, then, is both means and end, both process and purpose. It is a condition for and a characteristic of the evolutionary process in its thrust toward fulfillment; spiritual freedom is also the fullest completion of that process in its transcendent state as cosmic participation and supramental existence.

The recommended means to foster and achieve the full unfolding of the possibilities of spiritual freedom is integral yoga, whereby one enters into the "within" of one's deepest and secret self and there discovers spiritual resources previously untapped. Through yogic concentration and renunciation, the individual disciplines innate desires and intensifies the capacity for self-surrender to the divine, thus entering into full spiritual freedom with its consequent sense of oneness with all beings.

Aurobindo experienced his commitment to work for the larger liberation of humanity as a development of his concern for India's political growth; though he did not speak out frequently on public political issues at this time, he did express his interpretation of the forces operative during World War II and made specific procedural recommendations. Sensing a nonreceptive atmosphere, he concentrated on spiritual rather than temporal means ever more deeply, and understood India's eventual independence of 1947 as an act of divine determination far more than political victory.

Relating this discussion to the three levels of ethical analysis, it can be said that the triple transformation elucidated in Aurobindo's writings was concretely and historically begun in his exercise of yoga. In his own life this yoga had been begun during his Baroda days, was continued amid his political activity, and was concentrated on and deepened at Pondicherry. This yogic discipline brought about the first or psychic transformation from surface bodily existence to inner existence. The second or spiritual transformation occurred November 24, 1926, Aurobindo's day of *siddhi* or perfection, when he experienced the descent of the overmind, which in turn assured him that the supermind would descend without doubt; for the function of the overmind is to enable people to rise to supramental levels of consciousness.[83] This certitude was realized when the Mother announced the arrival of the supermind in April 1956.[84]

As Aurobindo admits, these experiences were the source of his insight and his pen flowed easily as he recorded the intensity and complexity of the meanings he received from above and from within. These articulated meanings themselves gave rise to prescriptive statements in which he invited and encouraged all people to be open to the supramental and to help hasten its worldwide expression. This is to be done through the effort and surrender that characterize integral yoga.

Given Aurobindo's emphasis on the meaning of freedom as the power to grow, to expand, to extend one's consciousness according to the inner (divine) law of one's being,[85] a further, though closely related question emerges and calls for attention. At what point does the individual's growth in freedom collide with the freedom of others, either restricting the freedom of the other or being restricted itself? In a word, how does Aurobindo handle the ever-challenging question of the relationship between the individual and society? Chapter 5 faces this question.

Notes

1. Letter to Joseph Baptista from Aurobindo, dated January 5, 1920, in *On Himself*, 26:429-30.

2. *Ibid.*, pp. 36-37.

3. *Ibid.*, p. 430.

4. *Sri Aurobindo Mandir Annual*, no. 26 (August 15, 1967), p. 126.

5. *On Himself*, 26:55.

6. "Karma and Freedom" (1915) in *The Supramental Manifestation*, 16:133-45.

7. See also "Rebirth and Karma," in *Supramental Manifestation*, 16:153-61, especially pp. 158-59 on the question of the role of heredity.

8. "Karma and Freedom," in *Supramental Manifestation*, 16:135.

9. *Ibid.*, p. 139.

10. *Ibid.*

11. *Ibid.*, p. 141.

12. *Ibid.*

13. *The Life Divine*, 19:900.

14. *Ibid.*, pp. 989-99.

15. "Karma and Freedom," in *Supramental Manifestation*, 16:143.

16. *Ibid.*, p. 144.

17. *Ibid.*

18. *Ibid.*, p. 145. In "The Terrestrial Law," in *Supramental Manifestation*, 16:187, Aurobindo summarizes this discussion aptly: "Man's relation with vital Nature is, again, first to be one with it by observance and obedience to its rule, then to know and direct it by conscious intelligence and will and to transcend by that direction the first law of life, its rule and habit, formula, initial significance."

Aurobindo treats the same theme of freedom and determinism, individual will and universal will similarly in other essays. See "Karma, Will and Consequence," in *Supramental Manifestation*, 16:146-52; "The Determinism of Nature," in *Essays on the Gita*, 13:202-13; "All-Will and Free-Will," in *Supramental Manifestation*, 16:282-86.

19. *Social and Political Thought*, 15:599.

20. *Ibid.*, p. 598.

21. *Ibid.*, p. 599.

22. *Ibid.*, p. 601.

23. *Life Divine*, 19:882.

24. *Ibid.*, p. 978. On the difference between the spiritual and the supramental, see also *On Himself*, 26:111. In the *Synthesis of Yoga*, 20:13, Aurobindo writes, "liberation is surely imperfect if it is only an escape and there is no return upon the containing substance and activities to exact and transform them."

25. *Life Divine*, 19:986.

26. *Ibid.*, pp. 997-98. On p. 1002 he words the highest law to which the seeker is called by the divine: "'Abandon all dharmas, all standards and rules of being and action, and take refuge in Me alone,'" See also pp. 1064-65.

27. *Ibid.*, p. 998; see also pp. 999-1000:

In the gnostic life, therefore, there is an entire accord between the free self-expression of the being and his automatic obedience to the inherent law of the supreme and universal Truth of things. These are to him interconnected sides of the one Truth; it is his own supreme truth of being which works itself out in the whole united truth of himself and things in one Supernature. There is also an entire accord between all the many and different powers of the being and their action; for even those that are contradictory in their apparent motion and seem in our mental experience of them to enter into conflict, fit themselves and their action naturally into each other, because each has its self-truth and its truth of relation to the others and this is self-found and self-formed in the gnostic Supernature.

Also p. 1006:

There would be no question of selfishness or altruism, of oneself and others, since all are seen and felt as the one self and only what the supreme Truth and Good decided would be done.

28. *Ibid*. Although Aurobindo also refers here to an "absolute freedom of infinity" characteristic of "the Absolute" at "the summit of being," it is not within the scope of this study to focus on the nature of the Divine within Aurobindo's metaphysics; consequently, neither will it detail this allusion of an absolute freedom as characteristic of the Absolute. See also *Synthesis of Yoga*, 20:43, where Aurobindo alludes to the divine existence as being of the nature of freedom. In *Die Philosophie von Sri Aurobindo im Hinblick auf Person* (Munich, 1965), pp. 41-43, 51-52, Günther Rager speaks to this issue briefly.

29. *Life Divine*, 19:1069-70.

30. *Ibid.*, p. 1027.

31. *Letters on Yoga*, 22:233.

32. See for example, "Planes and Parts of the Being," in *Letters on Yoga*, 22:269.

33. *Life Divine*, 19:854.

34. *Dictionary*, p. 195.

35. *Life Divine*, 19:1027.

36. *Synthesis of Yoga*, 20:4.

37. *Ibid.*, p. 28; see also *Synthesis of Yoga*, 21:583-84.

38. *Ibid.*, p. 584.

39. *Synthesis of Yoga*, 20:39. For documentation illustrating this contrast in approach from sources external to Aurobindo himself, see David Johnson, *Aurobindo Ghose*, p. 105, n7 (cited above, chap. 3, n7).

40. *Synthesis of Yoga*, 20:40-42.

41. *Letters on Yoga*, 22:251.

42. Even at the supramental level, however, ongoing divine progression or infinite development is possible. *Ibid*.

43. *Synthesis of Yoga*, 20:24; also p. 44, where Aurobindo comments that it is this thrust of his yoga that has traditionallly been the dream and hope of all the world's religions.

44. *Ibid.*, p. 50.

45. See *ibid.*, pp. 55,51.

46. *Ibid.*, p. 51.

47. *Ibid.*, p. 53.

48. *Ibid.* Yet as Aurobindo writes elsewhere, this surrender itself must be the free act of a living, choosing being and not a mechanical imposition from without, which would be merely the relative freedom he describes. See *Synthesis of Yoga*, 20:88.

49. *Ibid.*, p. 53. On Divine Grace, see *Letters on Yoga*, 23:607-11; *The Mother*, 25:1.

50. *Synthesis of Yoga*, 20:55. For the yogi young in the art, however, the experience and inspiration of the master is indispensable. See *On Himself*, 26:97.

51. *Synthesis of Yoga*, 20:80.

52. *Ibid.*, p. 62; also, see p. 267.

53. *Ibid.*, p. 68.

54. *Ibid.*, pp. 84-85. Although Aurobindo's yoga goes beyond the yoga of the Gita, he makes it clear that he esteems the Bhagavad Gita highly, for it is the source of "the most perfect system of Karmayoga known to man in the past." *Ibid.*, p. 87. See also *Essays on the Gita*, vol. 13.

55. See *Synthesis of Yoga*, 20:308-10.

56. *Life Divine*, 19:855.

57. *Ibid.*, also p. 856. A passage particularly pertinent here is the description of spirituality on p. 857:

spirituality is not a high intellectuality, not idealism, not an ethical turn of mind or moral purity and austerity, not religiosity or an ardent and exalted emotional fervour, not even a compound of all these excellent things; a mental belief, creed or faith, an emotional aspiration, a regulation of conduct according to a religious or ethical formula are not spiritual achievement and experience. These things are of considerable value to mind and life; they are of value to the spiritual evolution itself as preparatory movements disciplining, purifying or giving a suitable form to the nature; but they still belong to the mental evolution,—the beginning of a spiritual realisation, experience, change is not yet there. Spirituality is in its essence an awakening to the inner reality of our being, to a spirit, self, soul which is other than our mind, life and body, an inner aspiration to know, to feel, to be that, to enter into contact with the greater Reality beyond and pervading the universe which inhabits also our own being, to be in communion with It and union with It, and a turning, a conversion, a transformation of our whole being as a result of the aspiration, the contact, the union, a growth or waking into a new becoming or new being, a new self, a new nature.

58. *Ibid.*, p. 858.

59. *Synthesis of Yoga*, 20:310.

60. *Ibid.*, p. 314.

61. *Ibid.* In *Evolution and Religion: A Study in Sri Aurobindo and Pierre Teilhard de Chardin* (Oxford: Clarendon Press, 1971), Robert Charles Zaehner

illustrates Aurobindo and Teilhard's mutual concern to reinterpret their traditions in a way that brings out an essential concern with this world. See also Beatrice Bruteau, "Sri Aurobindo and Teilhard de Chardin on the Problem of Action," *International Philosophical Quarterly* 12, no. 2 (June 1972):193-204.

62. *Synthesis of Yoga*, 20:314-15. Aurobindo continues this description graphically:

> attachment and desire must be utterly cast out; there is nothing in the world to which we must be attached, not wealth nor poverty, nor joy nor suffering, nor life nor death, nor greatness nor littleness, nor vice nor virtue, nor friend, nor wife, nor children, nor country, nor our work and mission, nor heaven nor earth, nor all that is within them or beyond them. And this does not mean that there is nothing at all that we shall love, nothing in which we shall take delight; for attachment is egoism in love and not love itself, desire is limitation and insecurity in a hunger for pleasure and satisfaction and not the seeking after the divine delight in things. A universal love we must have, calm and yet eternally intense beyond the brief vehemence of the most violent passion; a delight in things rooted in a delight in God that does not adhere to their forms but to that which they conceal in themselves and that embraces the universe without being caught in its meshes.

63. *Ibid.*, p. 380; see also p. 425.

64. *Ibid.*, p. 88.

65. *Ibid.*, p. 90.

66. *Ibid.*, pp. 89-90.

67. *Ibid.*, p. 90; see also p. 374: "We have to realise the true self of ourselves and of all; and to realise the true self is to realise Sachchidananda."

68. *Synthesis of Yoga*, 21:594.

69. *Ibid.*, p. 602; see also p. 604.

70. *Ibid.*, 20:180; on the role and inadequacy of the ethical sphere see also pp. 142-45, 190-95, 417.

71. *Ibid.*, p. 208.

72. *Ibid.*, pp. 195-96; 21:614-15.

73. *Ibid.*, 20:164; also 490-91.

74. *Ibid.*, 21:587; also 596.

75. *Ibid.*, p. 588.

76. *Correspondence with Sri Aurobindo*, 1st comb. ed. (Pondicherry: Sri Aurobindo Ashram, 1969), p. 18.

77. *On Himself*, 26:196.

78. Nirodbaran, *Talks with Sri Aurobindo*, p. 44; A. B. Purani, *Evening Talks with Sri Aurobindo*, 2nd series (Pondicherry: Sri Aurobindo Ashram Press, 1961), p. 263; Mitra, *Liberator*, p. 214. In 1947, Aurobindo claimed that the force he used in world affairs was not that of the supramental but that of the overmind; its merely partial aspect is due to its getting entangled in the lower

forces of life and not being so pure nor powerful as supermind. *On Himself*, 26:170.

79. Mitra, *Liberator*, pp. 218-19; see also *On Himself*, 26:39.

80. Two versions of the text are available in *On Himself*, 26:400-406.

81. On July 7, 1947, Aurobindo wrote: " . . . I am getting a birthday present of a free India on August 15, but complicated by its being presented in two packets as two free Indias: this is a generosity I could have done without, one free India would have been enough for me if offered as an unbroken whole" (*On Himself*, 26:170-71).

82. *On Himself*, 26:172.

83. See Robert McDermott, "Sri Aurobindo: An Integrated Theory of Individual and Historical Transformation," *International Philosophical Quarterly* 12, no. 2 (June 1972): 177. Also Mitra, *Liberator*, p. 201. For a detailed account of the day of *siddhi*, see Purani, *Life*, pp. 214-21.

84. Mitra, *Liberator*, p. 279. Also McDermott, "An Integrated Theory," p. 177.

85. *The Human Cycle*, 15:170.

5

The Individual and Society

In an early Bengali writing, Aurobindo asserts a conviction that "man is not born for the society—but the society is created for him."[1] Yet in other early works he admits circumstances that point out the right of the nation over the individual. In "The Morality of Boycott," he makes a claim that it is to be expected that the nation will interfere with personal liberty.

> The whole of politics is an interference with personal liberty. Law is such an interference; protection is such an interference; the rule which makes the will of the majority prevail is such an interference. The right to prevent such use of personal liberty as will injure the interests of the race, is the fundamental law of society.[2]

And in "The Doctrine of Sacrifice" Aurobindo affirms the need for individuals to sacrifice themselves for the cause of the nation. It is only through sacrifice—on the part of the individual, the family, and the class—that "the supreme object of building up the nation" can occur.[3]

The context for these two latter excerpts is Aurobindo's nationalist cause. He sees two stages in the life of a nation: first, the process of formation; second, its organized formulation with position and power. It is during the first stage of becoming formed or reformed that the greatest demands are placed on the individual. At this stage the individual is called to self-sacrifice for the sake of the nation.[4]

In later (post-1910) writings, Aurobindo comments on the relationship between the individual and the community in a context that defines the individual as the fundamental starting point. For him the individual is "the key of the evolutionary movement"; the community finds its meaning in terms of the individuals who compose it and give it direction.

> The movement of the collectivity is a largely subconscious mass-movement; it has to formulate and express itself through the individuals to become conscious: its general mass-consciousness is always less evolved than the consciousness of its most developed individuals, and it progresses in so far as it accepts their impress or develops what they develop.[5]

The individual's commitment and loyalty are due not to the state nor to the community but to "the Truth, the Self, the Spirit, the Divine," whom one is to discover and disclose for oneself and the good of all.[6]

It is in *The Human Cycle* and *The Ideal of Human Unity* (originally *Arya* sequences, 1915-1918) that we find Aurobindo's more developed and explicit reflections on this question of the relationship between the individual and society as prompted by the larger question of freedom within the spiritual evolution.

Basing his thought on the categories of Lamprecht, Aurobindo gives them new meaning as he outlines the psychological evolution of human society according to five stages: symbolic, typal, conventional, individualistic, and subjective.[7]

The *symbolic* stage characterizes the primitive or early phase of a people who express themselves in imaginative and religious forms. The symbols of a primitive people speak of their experience of some presence behind life and life's activities. That presence can be seen as the divine, as a god, as the unnamable mystery of life. In India the Vedic period embodies this stage with its religious and spiritual world view.

The *typal* stage begins to emerge when the psychological and ethical forces surface and the spiritual-religious emphases recede to a position of sanctioning the ethical motivations and expectations. The risk run at this stage is the loss of the spiritual altogether and its substitution by convention. The *conventional* stage is born when the outward expression of values and ideals becomes more significant than the values or ideals themselves. The evolution of the caste system exhibits this change: what once had been an expression of reverence for learning (the Brahmin), for courage and strength (the Kshatriya), for financial productivity and fidelity (the Vaishya), for obedience and service (the Shudra), degenerated into a fixed social status. The conventional stage of a society fixes, systematizes, makes rigid. It is evident in Catholic monastic structures as well as in the Hindu caste structures.

The *individualistic* age occurs as a reaction against the failure of the conventional age and is "an attempt to get back from the conventionalism of belief and practice to some solid bed-rock, no matter what, of real and tangible Truth." People realize that "the Truth is dead in them and that they are living by a lie" (15:11). As a result, they question and they deny. In Europe the individualistic age began as a revolt of reason and eventually evolved to become a triumph of scientific achievement. Here the questioning turned on a variety of institutions: on a church heavy with a tradition that imposed itself; on politics, which laid claim to divine rights and privileges legitimating tyranny over the people; on social structures, which favored the high and exploited the low. And this questioning grew into a denial of the authority each field claimed to wield. Because any individualistic stage in history is rich with the risk of total chaos and confusion, it needs to be evened by a co-presence of two values: a generally recognizable standard of truth and a principle of social order that compels allegiance by the power of conviction from within and not by force from without. The discoveries of physical science satisfied this demand.

Yet Aurobindo envisions the coming of a new period in the human cycle of development. Physical science is more and more being seen to be incomplete as psychological and psychic phenomena continue to compel our attention and provide new questions about who we are. The emphasis on rationalism also is increasingly recognized as an incomplete entry into the meaning of human life; Nietzsche's will-to-live, Bergson's intuition, the German philosophical orientation to a suprarational sphere of truth are examples of this new thrust.

What the age of individualism has contributed to life is the realization that the individual is not simply a social unit.

He is not merely a member of a human pack, hive or anthill; he is something in himself, a soul, a being, who has to fulfil his own individual truth and law as well as his natural or his assigned part in the truth and law of the collective existence. (15:20)

Consequently, the individual demands in his or her very being space and freedom, room for initiative to grow to the fullest of possibilities. One cannot achieve this growth if dominated by others; one must turn to some source beyond the self.

The rationalistic current of thought has begun to be challenged by a growing *subjectivism*. Not at all clear in its contour, this newly emergent phase is a tentative and groping attempt to give shape to a new spirit. In this lies the hope for humanity, in the "infant and as yet subordinate tendencies which carry in them the seed of a new subjective and psychic dealing of man with his own being, with his fellow-men and with the ordering of his individual and social life (15:27). The newly emerging subjective spirit is most expressive "in the new collective self-consciousness of man in that organic mass of his life which he has most firmly developed in the past, the nation" (15:28).

"The primal law and purpose of the individual life is to seek its own self-development." Whether consciously or not, the individual strives to discover and to fulfill its true self, which is that of a "self-manifesting spirit" (15:29). So too, the "primal law and purpose of a society, community or nation is to seek its own self-fulfilment . . . ." The society or community, like the individual, is a living being, an expression of the eternal truth, a "self-manifestation of the cosmic Spirit" (15:29). Both the individual and society have in common many characteristics: "a body, an organic life, a moral and aesthetic temperament, a developing mind and a soul . . . ." These common elements are more than analogues or parallels. To Aurobindo there is a "real identity of nature" between the two (15:29).

The differences, however, cannot be ignored, and Aurobindo admits their reality.[8] The group-soul is far more complex and must go through a more difficult and lengthier process in finding itself. Ordinarily the nation names itself in terms of geographical boundaries based on land identification. This is its objective aspect. But only when we begin to feel that its more real identity comes from the people who compose it are we growing into a genuinely subjective appreciation that its deeper meaning resides in its communal consciousness.[9]

The *objective* view of life is rationalistic and analytical, taking an external and mechanical view of things, seeing the world as a thing, an object to be studied by observation from without. It views the state as an entity in itself apart from the community and the individuals who compose it, with a right to impose its laws and values on them. Life is to be managed, mechanized, and even manipulated; the law is outside the self and demands conformity. The *subjective* view of life, in contrast, values the law that is within the self and regards everything from the perspective of a developing self-consciousness. Life is seen as a self-creating process; its principle of progress is that of an increasing self-recognition, self-discovery, and self-invention. It values the many powers of human life beyond mere reason and will and emphasizes the intuitional process of knowing; its main emphasis is to come in touch with the self, living and seeing out of an internal center.[10]

Aurobindo values the subjective appreciation wherein a nation sees itself as a living organism that has a right to pursue its own growth and development; he decries an objectivist reduction to externals.[11] Yet he admits that the subjective understanding runs the risk of several dangerous illusions itself. The Germany of World War I embodies the collective self-consciousness and exhibits a newly emergent subjectivism. And yet its "first enormous stumble" was to translate the error of individualistic egoism into communal egoism.[12]

Just as the individual must break through the illusion of his own ultimate importance to realize that his real self is not the ego but the divine individuality, and just as one must break through the illusion of absolute independence to discover interdependence and solidarity with all of one's kind, so too, the nation must come to similar realizations, namely, that its visible body is not its true self and that it is not intended to live in isolated self-esteem but rather for the good of the rest of the world.

In these two attributes of genuine subjectivism Germany erred. Germany saw its "collective ego" as "the greatest actual organised expression of life" to which everything else was to be subservient, and also "saw the individual merely as a cell of the collective ego."[13]

From this perspective of egoistic self-concern, three conclusions follow, each destructive in its impact. First, because the individual is seen merely as a cell in the larger collective organism, its life is completely subservient to the efficiency of the nation. The nation educates and initiates; the individual obeys and executes. The cult of the state begun by Germany in the modern period induced the effacement of the individual. Second, because of the dominance of the society and the subservience of the individual, the state becomes the sole absolute rule of morality, a morality based on power and therefore on war, efficiency, and productivity. Third, whatever is, is to be assimilated into this culture, and whatever is resistant is to be eliminated.[14]

Thus, according to Aurobindo's interpretation, in the name of rediscovering the subjective awareness of itself as a nation, Germany gave in to a gross materialism. "Thus she arrived at a bastard creed, an objective subjectivism which is miles apart from the true goal of a subjective age."[15] For Aurobindo that "true goal" is rooted not in the egoism of physical, economic, or cultural life, but in "a Self one in difference which relates the good of each, on a footing of equality and not of strife and domination, to the good of the rest of the world" (15:47).

The coming in touch with this Self is achieved primarily through the individual through whom the divine manifests itself. Yet this growth into realizing one's divine destiny is intensely communal as well as individual, for perfection or fulfillment is named in terms of world fulfillment and not merely in terms of a "lonely salvation" (15:58).

> The object of society then is basically twofold: . . .first to provide the conditions of life and growth by which individual Man,—not isolated men or a class or a privileged race, but all individual men according to their capacity,—and the race through the growth of its individuals may travel towards this divine perfection. It must be, secondly, as mankind generally more and more grows near to some figure of the Divine in life and more and more men arrive at it,—for the cycles are many and each cycle has its own figure of the Divine in man,—to express in the general life of mankind, the light, the power, the beauty, the harmony, the joy of the Self that has been attained and that pours itself out in a freer and nobler humanity. (15:58)

Again we find freedom and unity to be the fundamental values in

Aurobindo's framework. Freedom of the individual, freedom of the group, freedom of the race, together with a unity of "co-ordinated harmony" of the individual's forces, the group's efforts, and those of the various races across the globe (15:58-59).

Humankind is the primary expression of the divine's cosmic self-disclosure. Yet it is up to each individual human being to come in touch with this divine disclosure and he must do it according to the lines of his own pattern of development; he must seek this growth from within. Only then will his discovery and fulfillment be profound, alive, and deeply rooted. Though his life and growth are for the sake of the world, his impact will have value only to the extent that he is in touch with his deepest and real self, encouraging, allowing, aiding that self (15:60).

Many instruments are available to help make this process real progress: the laws, disciplines, and ideals of both past ages and the present age. But even these external guides must be relative to the principle of each one's own nature and the call of the future. Whatever the specific type (church, class, association, nation, etc.), communities function to mediate the individual and humanity, helping each to complete the other. And so a community that places an absolute claim on its individual members is an aberration from the truth just as much as an individual's decision to live egoistically in isolation and/or self-concern is an aberration from the truth (15:62).

In a somewhat lengthy but key paragraph, Aurobindo states his position with respect to the law of the individual, the law of the community, and the law of humanity.

> Thus the law for the individual is to perfect his individuality by free development from within, but to respect and to aid and be aided by the same free development in others. His law is to harmonise his life with the life of the social aggregate and to pour himself out as a force for growth and perfection on humanity. The law for the community or nation is equally to perfect its corporate existence by a free development from within, aiding and taking full advantage of that of the individual, but to respect and to aid and be aided by the same free development of other communities and nations. Its law is to harmonise its life with that of the human aggregate and to pour itself out as a force for growth and perfection on humanity. The law for humanity is to pursue its upward evolution towards the finding and expression of the

Divine in the type of mankind, taking full advantage of the free development and gains of all individuals and nations and groupings of men, to work towards the day when mankind may be really and not only ideally one divine family, but even then, when it has succeeded in unifying itself, to respect, aid and be aided by the free growth and activity of its individuals and constituent aggregates. (15:63-64)

Admitting the idealism of this vision and the struggle of the human attempt to attain it, Aurobindo feels it may indeed be possible. For his perception is consonant with the impulse of the subjective phase of social development and he discerns glimpses of its presence in current history.

It is within Aurobindo's interpretation of life's highest value as that of the discovery and expression of the divine[16] that he offers a criticism of other ethical systems. He finds nineteenth-century utilitarianism weak in its practical and external, almost mathematical concern with useful results. So too, hedonistic ethical theory errs in referring virtue to pleasure, satisfaction, or social impulses. Aurobindo admits that each of these theories has some hold on reality. Utility is a value, a "fundamental principle of existence and . . .the highest good is also the highest utility" (15:139). Furthermore the good of all is precisely the aim of both Aurobindo's metaphysical and yoga systems. Yet utility does not function to regulate ethical decision-making but provides only one consideration among many other considerations. "Good, not utility, must be the principle and standard of good; otherwise we fall into the hands of that dangerous pretender expedience, whose whole method is alien to the ethical" (15:139).

Even pleasure is a value if seen as the highest bliss (ananda) or delight of being. But pleasure is no test or standard for decision-making. For Aurobindo there is a single rule for the ethical person to follow and that is "his principle of good, his instinct for good, his vision of good, his intuition of good." This is the law of his nature; it cannot be in utility nor in pleasure. "The action of the ethical man is not motived by even an inner pleasure, but by a call of his being, the necessity of an ideal, the figure of an absolute standard, a law of the Divine" (15:140).

Though the demands and pressures of social interaction give rise to the individual ethical decision-making process, the heart of the ethical struggle is rooted in one's openness to God. One's relationships with oneself and with others are "the occasions of his ethical growth; but that which determines his ethical being is his relations with God, the urge of the Divine upon him whether concealed in his nature or conscious in his higher self or inner genius." In brief, "the ethical imperative comes not from around, but from within him and above him" (15:141).

The ideals presented by democratic individualism as a way of life, and democratic socialism as well, further illustrate the inadequacy of recent social structures. Since the practice of the democratic ideal exhibits the rule of one group over another, strife and struggle, conflict and competition among classes reign rampant. Even the emphasis on education and freedom (admitted goods in themselves) have too often been overwhelmed by the scramble for power and wealth, and become stimulants to continuous competition and conflict (15:185-87).

Democratic socialism, as a reaction against capitalism, has also expressed itself in a war of classes; furthermore, it has taken on a highly industrial and economic tone, which disfigures its true impulse to destroy the competitive thrust that can be so destructive to human life. Since it presupposes perfect social equality as its basis, it runs the risk of seeing the individual only as a member of the society and for the sake of society. The individual's identity becomes submerged in the collectivity (15:187-89).

Yet the impulse for freedom and equality is rooted in the individual. The individual longs for and demands space, time, opportunity to expand and grow and be honored as well as any other. It is only the third member of the "democratic trinity" known as brotherhood, fraternity, or comradeship, that can survive on the level of the social grouping. But without liberty or equality, fraternity loses its strength, dissolving into a thin association of units sharing together only a "common service to the life of the nation under the absolute control of the collectivist State" (15:191).

In *The Ideal of Human Unity* as well as *The Human Cycle*, Aurobindo focuses on this theme also, pointing to the intrinsically necessary relationship among liberty, equality, and fraternity. Without a lived interconnectedness, a variety of destructive directions takes place.

When the ego claims liberty, it arrives at competitive individualism.

> When it asserts equality, it arrives first at strife, then . . .constructs an artificial and machine-made society. (15:546)

What is true of the individual ego is also true of the group ego:

> A society that pursues liberty as its ideal is unable to achieve equality; a society that aims at equality will be obliged to sacrifice liberty. For the ego to speak of fraternity is for it to speak of something contrary to its nature. (15:546)

Aurobindo resolves this dilemma by appealing to his fundamental conviction that spirit is at the heart of being and value, and that in the spirit alone does his hope rest for a balanced rhythm of both individual and communal dimensions of life. Though for Aurobindo spirit is that which transcends human existence, spirit is also that which affirms and fulfills human life. There all human powers and possibilities are accepted; rational, aesthetic, ethical, emotional, interpersonal, material, and physical. In a spiritualized society alone does the hope for the achievement of individual and communal fulfillment become a real possibility.[17] And this will come about only through a transformation of an individual and eventually of many individuals,[18] a transformation that involves a transference of the center of life from mental consciousness and power to a higher supramental consciousness and power.[19]

Fraternity is a thing of the spirit; without fraternity neither liberty nor equality can be constructive.

> brotherhood is the real key to the triple gospel of the idea of humanity. The union of liberty and equality can only be achieved by the power of human brotherhood and it cannot be founded on anything else. But brotherhood exists only in the soul and by the soul; it can exist by nothing else.[20]

This soul-power of brotherhood is only fully realized in the supramental realm of divine consciousness in which full freedom and unity are achieved. In turn, a spiritual society would express itself with a concern to make the divine discoverable in its entire range of activities, educational, economic, artistic, and the like.[21]

It would also be concerned with fostering and honoring the "within" of every individual, diminishing as fully as possible any hint of "external compulsion," encouraging only the awakening of "the inner divine compulsion of the Spirit within."[22]

> For the perfectly spiritualised society will be one in which, as is dreamed by the spiritual anarchist, all men will be deeply free, and it will be so because the preliminary condition will have been satisfied. In that state each man will be not a law to himself, but *the* law, the divine law, because he will be a soul living in the Divine and not an ego living merely if not entirely for its own interest and purpose. His life will be led by the law of his own divine nature liberated from the ego.[23]

Collectively this takes shape in what Aurobindo calls the "religion of humanity," which is defined neither by system nor by creed, nor by dogma nor rite. (Religions so defined, he notes, have all failed in the past.)

> A religion of humanity means the growing realisation that there is a secret Spirit, a divine Reality, in which we are all one, that humanity is its highest present vehicle on earth, that the human race and the human being are the means by which it will progressively reveal itself here.[24]

This new religion of humanity brings with it the balanced reverence for liberty, equality, and brotherhood. Here the individual realizes that his own life is complete only in the life of other persons. And the human race itself realizes that its perfection can be found only in respecting and fostering the free and full life in the individual.[25] Clearly then, freedom and unity remain enduring values for Aurobindo. They are enduring since both are rooted in the spirit and since the spirit is one, yet varied and free in self-expression and self-manifestation.[26]

Concretely, historically, the question of the possibility of a religion of humanity poses itself—whether or not it is possible for humanity to transcend the current nation-unit, the now largest functioning collective grouping. Can an aggregate be formed that encloses many or all nations in a totality that honors the principles of self-determination and brotherhood simultaneously? Aurobindo's claim is that if we are to survive and to forward the evolutionary thrust for which we currently have responsibility, the chaos and conflict of international life must somehow be diminished and deflected into a new form of united action and harmonious living.[27]

Aurobindo absorbs something of each stage of societal evolution in his construction of the ideal society. He appreciates the tendency of the symbolic stage to look beyond the concreteness and immediacy of the moment to a deeper reality, hidden within yet discoverable if sought. The typal stage provides him with the ethical-psychological dimensions of life which, though not of absolute nor even central value, do nonetheless function in an instrumental way, aiding the total process. The conventional phase contributes the recognized need for forms and patterns of activity; the individual and subjective stages uncover the importance of the individual from the viewpoint of subjective appreciation in contrast to the results of an objective observational approach. In this way all points on the continuum illuminate the direction of the future ideal that Aurobindo anticipates as real possibility.[28]

The most recent phase of subjectivism is prelude to the coming of the spiritual age that Aurobindo envisions. For the spiritual change of which he speaks to be effected, however, two conditions must be satisfied simultaneously. On the one hand there must be individuals who share his vision and who structure their lives in the image of the spirit, exemplifying for others a truly viable and valuable style of living.

On the other hand, in addition to these creative and visionary initiators, there must also be a readiness on the part of the larger community of humankind, a receptivity enabling the many to model themselves on the few.[29] Only when both conditions are met will the decisive spiritual change occur in a communal manner. Aurobindo's view of the future evolution of humanity can begin with a single person, and in fact, has so begun. However, because of his perspective that the future stage is a collective stage, the environment itself becomes crucial in making the future come about. Aurobindo is confident that such a future stage will occur because the evolution of consciousness takes place according to a *law* of advancing consciousness. It is according to this law that consciousness itself will be unified and that the *future supramental age* will occur.[30] Yet, because the supermind does not impose itself upon human life, its eventual manifestation depends upon the willingness of human beings to be open to and to receive the divine. In this relationship of the supramental to the mental, and of the future to the present, we see that both grace and effort are necessary. In this way, Aurobindo attempts to resolve the tension between determinism and liberty.

Notes

1. "A Word About Society," trans. Niranjan, *Sri Aurobindo Mandir Annual*, no. 26 (August 15, 1967), p. 106.

2. *Bande Mataram*, 1:127.

3. *Karmayogin*, 2:110.

4. *Ibid.*, pp. 109-10.

5. *Life Divine*, 19:1050.

6. *Ibid.*

7. *Human Cycle*, in *Social and Political Thought*, 15:2. The following discussion explaining these five stages is drawn from pp. 2-28.

8. See also *Ideal of Human Unity, ibid.*, pp. 272-77, and *Life Divine*, 19:1046-51.

9. *Human Cycle*, in *Social and Political Thought*, 15:30.

10. *Ibid.*, pp. 50-52.

11. See also *Ideal of Human Unity, ibid.*, p. 404: "Carried too far, an imposed order discourages the principle of natural growth which is the true method of life and may even slay the capacity for real growth . . . . Better anarchy than the long continuance of a law which is not our own or which our real nature cannot assimilate . . . . Human society progresses really and vitally in proportion as law becomes the child of freedom . . . ."

12. *Human Cycle, ibid.*, p. 38.

13. *Ibid.*, p. 41.

14. *Ibid.*, pp. 42-44. Also *Ideal of Human Unity, ibid.*, pp. 278-84, on the inadequacy of the state.

15. *Human Cycle, ibid.*, p. 46.

16. "All life is only a lavish and manifold opportunity given us to discover, realise, express the Divine" (*ibid.*, p. 138).

17. *Human Cycle, ibid.*, pp. 171-72. Also on p. 170: "Spirituality respects the freedom of the human soul, because it is itself fulfilled by freedom; and the deepest meaning of freedom is the power to expand and grow towards perfection by the law of one's own nature, *dharma* . . . . It will give the same freedom to man's seeking for political and social perfection and to all his other powers and aspirations." See also p. 249: " . . . the nature of the Spirit is a spacious inner freedom and a large unity into which each man must be allowed to grow according to his own nature."

18. *Ibid.*, pp. 231-32.

19. *Ibid.*, pp. 226-27.

20. *Ideal of Human Unity, ibid.*, pp. 546-47.

21. *Human Cycle, ibid.*, p. 240. See pp. 241-42 for a fuller sketch of what this spiritualized society would look like. See also *Ideal of Human Unity* for Aurobindo's hope regarding the possibility of a world union that would be based on free self-determination rather than on war, in which "unity would be the largest principle of life, but freedom would be its foundation-stone" (*ibid.*, p. 517). For an introduction to Auroville, a new city just outside Pondicherry begun under the auspices of the Mother to express Aurobindo's vision, see *Cross Currents*, ed. Robert McDermott, 22, no. 1 (Winter 1972): 67-111 and *Auroville: The First Six Years 1968-1974* (Auroville, India: Auropublication, n.d.).

22. *Human Cycle, ibid.*, p. 243.

23. *Ibid.*

24. *Ideal of Human Unity, ibid.*, p. 554.

25. *Ibid.* See also *War and Self-Determination, ibid.*, pp. 606-7.

26. *Ideal of Human Unity, ibid.*, p. 554.

27. *Ibid.*, pp. 562-63. Also *War and Self-Determination, ibid.*, p. 587. For fuller studies of Aurobindo's social philosophy and psychology, see: Kishor Gandhi, *Social Philosophy and the New Age* (Pondicherry: Sri Aurobindo Society, 1965); N. V. Subbannachar, *Social Psychology: the Integral Approach* (Calcutta: Scientific Book Agency, 1966); Vishwanath Prasad Varma, *The Political Philosophy of Sri Aurobindo* (cited earlier), which is a reconstruction as well as an exposition of Aurobindo's thought.

Shorter, though insightful articles are also available. See Eugene Fontinell, "A Pragmatic Approach to THE HUMAN CYCLE," in *Six Pillars*, ed. McDermott, pp. 129-59; Grace E. Cairns, "Aurobindo's Conception of the Nature and Meaning of History," *International Philosophical Quarterly* 12, no. 2 (June 1972): 205-19; also John M. Koller, "Types of Society: The Social Thought of Sri Aurobindo," *ibid.*, 220-33.

28. John M. Koller, "Types of Society," pp. 232-33.

29. *Human Cycle*, in *Social and Political Thought*, 15: 231-45.

30. McDermott refers to the projected supramental age as a sixth stage in Aurobindo's outline of societal development; since *The Human Cycle* remains as it was written in 1918, we need to read these stages in the context of his completed works where the supramental is explicitly described. *The Essential Aurobindo*, ed. Robert A. McDermott (New York: Schocken, 1973), p. 168.

6

Conclusion

Given the initial interest that prompted this study, namely, to disclose Aurobindo's understanding and appreciation of political and spiritual freedom or liberation, this final chapter is written to reflect critically upon the major motifs disclosed in the expository chapters, to note the consistency between the metaethical perspective and his ethical prescriptions, to raise questions prompted by the study, and to examine the nature of the relationship between political freedom and spiritual freedom in his life and writings.

Law is a major motif pervading Aurobindo's essays and undergirding related themes such as the relationship between the divine and the human, the values of passive resistance and armed revolt, political, cultural, and spiritual freedom, and the deepest dimension of supramental gnostic existence. The theme of law has recurred in the discussions of earlier chapters, and can be assessed and appreciated now in relationship to other voices in the literature of liberation.

Law

Aurobindo appeals to divine law to legitimate his revolutionary stand during the political period and in this he resembles other twentieth-century revolutionary thinkers and activists of the Third World nations of Africa, Asia, and Latin America. In an article on the religious dimension in recent revolutionary literature and life, Donald Smith (of the University of Pennsylvania) observes that men such as Mahatma Gandhi,

Vinoba Bhave, and Camilo Torres give witness to this particular characteristic of revolutionary thought and action: religiosity.[1] Reinterpreting their religious traditions and appealing to the religious sensibilities of their people, they provide a sharp contrast to Marxist theories of revolution. Religion functions as referent, not in order to justify the oppressive regime and to level the masses into passive acceptance of the oppressor, but to prompt protest and to sanction active dissent against the domination of the oppressor.[2]

Aurobindo exhibits this religio-revolutionary style as well. David Johnson's study on the religious dimension in Aurobindo's early thought points to the limitation of his synthetic vision on the practical level precisely in terms of the religious quality in Aurobindo's appeal. Johnson maintains that the very symbols, metaphors, and events that profoundly touched and energized the Hindu masses excluded both the Muslim Indians and the British. The Muslins could not identify with the Hindu story. And the British could not accept the absoluteness of swaraj. Thus, Aurobindo failed to reach either, and as a consequence he was unable to achieve liberation for India.[3]

In response to Johnson's conclusion, however, it must be pointed out that, besides Aurobindo's appeal to the religious heritage of the Hindu people, with its emphasis on the divine will, divine commands, and divine law, Aurobindo appeals to another root in human life. He calls it the "law" of things, the "nature" of things, trying to get at the way things are. In a word, he appeals not only to divine law but to natural law.

His essay "The Right of Association" exemplifies this particularly clearly in its discussion of three fundamental human rights: free press, free public meeting, and free association. For Aurobindo these are so basic as to be indisputable. He observes that they are (at least theoretically) acknowledged in Europe itself and expressed in the continuing quest for liberty, equality, and fraternity. Whether embodied in the Buddha, the Christ, or a-religious humanism, for Aurobindo these values (particularly fraternity) reflect soul power.

In this we see his attempt to broaden the base of his religious references to humanistic values with which Indian Muslims and British Christians as well as Hindus would be able to identify.[4]

Both divine law and natural law become Aurobindo's base for justifying revolution and therefore for legitimating the refusal to obey social-political laws. At this point Aurobindo clearly speaks to the just-war, just-revolution debate as one of its advocates. In Richard J. Neuhaus's terms, Aurobindo is neither pacifist nor crusader but a discriminating, reflective revolutionary who endorses not only the legitimacy of revolution but the responsibility under certain conditions actually to bring it about.[5]

Aurobindo discriminates further by scrutinizing the means of revolutionary change. Both boycott and armed revolt are justified and are to be selected according to the intensity of pressure applied by the oppressor. When the situation is urgent and there is neither time to stall nor room to move due to the oppressor's force, violence becomes the fitting response. But where time is a given and the pressure less intense, a nonviolent means such as boycott is preferred, for it not only avoids bloodshed but contains within itself the desired goal of the revolution: life and liberty co-present.

In this regard Aurobindo is similar to Mahatma Gandhi and Martin Luther King, both of whom speak of the relationship between means and ends as a critical component of successful and ethical revolution. For Gandhi and King, the means were the end in process of becoming. Peaceful means alone were capable of creating a peaceful end. It is of the nature of violence to perpetuate itself, they felt, and only love is powerful enough to cut through the vicious circle of hate and thereby bring about the desired end: life characterized by love as well as liberty.[6]

Aurobindo's similarity to Gandhi and King at this juncture, however, refers solely to tactics and strategies, not to philosophical world view nor to ethical principles. In *Talks with Sri Aurobindo*, Nirodbaran, a disciple, records a conversation Aurobindo had with Purani on January 8, 1939, which illustrates Aurobindo's reservations about the realism of Gandhi's interpretation of nonviolence:

> P: . . . Gandhi writes that non-violence tried by some people in Germany has failed because it has not been so strong as to generate sufficient heat to melt Hitler's heart.
>
> SRI AUROBINDO: It would have to be a furnace in that case. The only way to melt his heart is to bomb it out of existence.[7]

Another conversation dated January 16, 1939, details more fully Aurobindo's disagreement with Gandhi's approach to passive resistance:

> SRI AUROBINDO: This idea of passive resistance I have never been able to fathom. I can understand an absolute non-resistance to evil, what the Christians mean when they say, "Resist not Evil." You may die without resisting and accept the consequences as sent by God. But to change the opponent's heart by passive resistance is something I don't understand.
>
> P: I agree with the *Modern Review* that by this method one allows evil to triumph. It seems foolish to expect that a *goonda's* heart will melt in that way.
>
> SRI AUROBINDO: Precisely. Gandhi has been trying to apply to ordinary life what belongs to spirituality. Non-violence or *ahimsa* as a spiritual attitude and practice is perfectly intelligible and has a standing of its own. You may not accept it *in toto* but it has a basis in Reality. To apply it to ordinary life is absurd. One then ignores—as the Europeans do in several things—the principle of *adhikarbheda* and the difference of situation.
>
> P: Gandhi's point is that in either case you die. If you die with arms you encourage and perpetuate the killing method.
>
> SRI AUROBINDO: And if you die without arms you encourage and perpetuate passive rsistance [*sic*]. (*Laughter*)
>
> It is certainly a principle which can be applied successfully if practiced on a mass-scale, specially by unarmed people like Indians. I understand this principle, because you, being unarmed, are left with no other choice. But even if it succeeds, it is not because you have changed the heart of the enemy but because you have made it impossible for him to rule.[8]

Where Gandhi (and King) absolutized suffering love as the means necessary to make the revolution happen both ethically and tactically, Aurobindo chose the strategies of nonviolent resistance solely on the basis of the results produced. Even his perception of suffering as a value was pragmatically oriented. He does not, for example, endorse the love ethic, which implicitly or explicitly exhorts people to "turn the other cheek" in the face of attack. Rather, his respect for suffering is due to its function of awakening India; he saw the pain of oppression prompt India to a new recognition of its status as an exploited people and to mobilize from within a new energy in refusing to perpetuate this status.

In spite of his slogan of "no compromise" to the British, the issue of the tax boycott also demonstrates that Aurobindo was no purist in the political arena but was quite willing to compromise. He admitted, for example, that a tax boycott would have been the fullest expression of refusal, the clearest way for India to withdraw support, to exercise her determination, to immobilize the alien power by forcing the British into economic crisis. But pragmatic political judgments moved him not to choose the tax boycott, because of the legal strength Britain still exercised, a strength that would inflict legal reprisals and jail sentences on masses of Indians, thus immobilizing their resistance activities.

Coextensive with Aurobindo's plan to have India refuse to submit to British law is his intention that with the same vigor India should refuse to be shaped by British consciousness and value perception. At this level it is clear that his sense of political freedom demands cultural freedom. Aurobindo warns his peers to beware of modeling themselves on Europe, and in this context he decries the inherent weakness of the West—its mechanistic, materialistic mentality. In this instance of warning Indians not to imitate Europe but to express their own deepest selves, Aurobindo shares convictions with Paulo Freire, Brazilian advocate and spokesman of the Latin American struggle for liberation.[9]

Freire comments that the temptation of revolutionaries struggling to free themselves and their people is to gain freedom by oppressing the former oppressor. The old oppressed become the new oppressors. The old oppressors become the new oppressed. Such a shift serves only to exchange personnel and consequently to continue to perpetuate a dehumanized and dehumanizing environment. The only change is that of role, for it does not offer new structures, new relationships, new anything. The dehumanizing process continues but now in opposite fashion. The revolution degenerates into mere role reversal. Freire's attempt to break through this circle of repetition comes in his understanding of liberation: neither gift from others nor achievement by oneself, liberation is both gift and self-achievement simultaneously. It is a mutual process wherein the oppressed and their leaders liberate one another and their oppressors as well. Freire maintains that, though the struggle for liberation is the task of the oppressed and must begin with their initiative, they must humanize their oppressors as they go, engaging them in dialogue, calling them from their inhumanity and challenging them to become more human. Pertinent to this point is the awareness that the oppressed must break through to a new consciousness that topples their current model of personhood imposed by the oppressor. For Freire this new model will emerge in ''the appearance of the new man: neither oppressor nor oppressed, but man in the process of liberation''[10]—persons in process of attaining their deepest ''ontological and historical vocation of becoming more fully human.''[11]

For Aurobindo too, since India is (at least in part) responsible for its own unfreedom, it must take the lead in saying no. Liberty is self-dependence, not British dependence. Because of a deep trust in the history and spirit of India, Aurobindo feels that India should be its own model for growth. Nothing external is to be emulated. Ultimately, as his later thought indicates, the more "within" he pressed, the more he realized that it was the vision of supermanhood that more accurately captured that hopeful model of human life. It is in this supramental consciousness to which India is called that Aurobindo's concepts of divine law and natural law come together. To partake of the supramental consciousness is to share in the divine nature and to be in touch with a reality neither alien nor apart, but to be in touch with one's own deepest self.

This divine-law/natural-law identification, however, is never identified with the laws of the British structured into Indian society. When Aurobindo entertains the possibility that Britain's role in Indian history might be in fact a part of India's divine dharma facilitating the evolutionary thrust, he does so not to manifest any openness to Britain, but to explain to his people that British rule came as a punishment from God due to their own passivity.[12]

Abstracting from British law to social law in general, Aurobindo's divine-law/natural-law identification is never identified with any social law and therefore never with Indian social law, for these laws are seen as temporary strictures necessary only while people remain at the mental stage of evolution, living in the Ignorance. Entry into the supramental gnostic stage of existence transcends the very need for social and ethical standards by dissolving the externally created norms and expectations of society through discovering the internal law or dynamic of one's own being now identified as the divine within. Supermanhood becomes the paradigm for human fulfillment; the gnostic being is supramental, supracategorical, and supraethical.

The Question of Consistency

As a fully articulated world view, Aurobindo's vision is brilliant in the comprehensiveness of both contour and content. Especially noteworthy is the consistency between its metaethical perspective and its concrete recommendations for life ("ethical prescriptions"). For example, Aurobindo's prescriptive statements exhorting Indians to trust and to love their own heritage, to throw off the shackles of British law and consciousness through refusal and resistance are recommendations rooted in several beliefs: that the divinity is manifest in the motherland, that external and alien laws are unjust and destructive, and that only that which grows from within is to be nourished and fostered as truly expressive of the divine. Furthermore, Aurobindo's invitation to us all to surrender to the divine through the discipline of integral yoga reflects his metaphysical conviction that life is marked by the evolution of the spirit and that spiritual power is available to all who open themselves to it. The behavioral recommendations flow from and give expression to his metaphysical principles.

Furthermore, Aurobindo's distinction between the mental plane and the supramental plane leads him to acknowledge the inherent limitations of the ethical realm due to its connection with the mental level of existence. Like the mental, the ethical is a necessary and important stage of evolutionary development, but a temporary phase at most. It is expected to be transcended. And so what we find in Aurobindo's thought is that, given his presuppositions, he is consistent in doing mental ethics for the mental plane of existence and supramental nonethics or supraethics for the supramental plane. Internally considered, Aurobindo's thought satisfies Smurl's good-story criterion of consistency.

From a position external to the system, however, two issues emerge and raise questions that call for attention. These issues are noted as difficulties I discover in the process of assessing and appropriating Aurobindo's thought.

Difficulties in the Dialogue

One difficulty is what I call the absence of a self-critical spirit regarding the epistemological presupposition that informs his thought. Aurobindo's experience is characterized by a powerful certitude. His journey to Pondicherry is the result of a "distinct adesh" (divine command), not a decision following reflection and considered conversation. The withdrawal following his public support of the Cripps proposal came from a realization that the public would not listen to him. Yet a question arises: would he listen to them either? Clearly not, for his knowledge was not derived from perceptions of the people; his convictions came to him directly from the divine. The question to be faced is: how does one distinguish divine insight from the creation of one's own truth?

Not to so distinguish, of course, is to reject the very possibility of illusion in perception. The spiritual visionary who is able to be self-critical, however, brings his or her certitude into dialogue with alternative perceptions and invites response. One might word the question in a variety of ways: What is the possibility that my certitude stems not from contact with the divine but from lack of contact with my own needs? What is the likelihood that my convictions are creations of my imagination rather than discoveries of the divine? Or how possible is it that my new understandings are distorted and are thereby closing me off from what is, rather than opening me to what is? How might I test my perceptions to judge their truthfulness, their goodness, their beauty? And so on.

These are but examples of self-critical questioning that reflect sufficient self-doubt to engage the mystic or spiritual person in the human struggle and search for truth and goodness, whereby one places oneself in a position of listening to many voices and not simply one voice, looking toward many sources rather than merely one. In this way the person trusts that the combination of sources (people past and present, known in person or contacted through literature, sense experience, intuitive insight, discursive thought, empirical proofs, in a word, everything available) will contain built-in correctives challenging, modifying, perhaps reinforcing those certitudes. Such a process of reflection need not dilute the mystic's bond with the divine nor dissolve one's sense of the absoluteness of the divine; it simply recognizes the relativity of human perception. Furthermore, it accepts that relativity both as fact of life and source of truth to be tapped in the total struggle. Does Aurobindo deal with these questions? How would he address one who does not share his certitude, or who trusts the many voices as source of wisdom rather than one voice understood as the divine?

In response to such questions, Aurobindo's claim, I believe, would be this: the spiritual search transcends the realm of rational or scientific inquiry; it is not possible to use the ordinary reason as an instrument for testing spiritual experience; nor can the ordinary reason determine whether such things are real, and if so, under what laws they exist. There is a process for testing, but it is not the process of ordinary reasoning and experiencing. It is a process of intuitive discrimination, which assesses spiritual experience in the light of one's guru, systems of the past, and the relationship of experience to experience. On November 18, 1934, Aurobindo described this testing process.

> As in Science, so here you have to accumulate experience on experience, following faithfully the methods laid down by the Guru or by the systems of the past, you have to develop an intuitive discrimination which compares the experiences, see what they mean, how far and in what field each is valid, what is the place of each in the whole, how it can be reconciled or related with others that at first might seem to contradict it, etc., etc., until you can move with a secure knowledge in the vast field of spiritual phenomena. That is the only way to test spiritual experience. I have myself tried the other method and I have found it absolutely incapable and inapplicable . . . . I am unable to see by what valid tests you propose to make the ordinary reason the judge of what is beyond it.[13]

Regarding his own spiritual experiences, Aurobindo accepted them in all their power, allowed them to have their full impact and, in time, was better able to discern their truth and worth.

> I did the only thing I could—to accept it as a strong and valid truth of experience, let it have its full play and produce its full experiential consequences until I had sufficient Yogic knowledge to put it in its place. Finally, how without inner knowledge or experience can you or anyone else test the inner knowledge and experience of others?[14]

From Aurobindo's point of view, one cannot judge the supramental vision from the mental perceptions or vital drives. Since the knowledge he valued most concerned the nature and the evolution of consciousness, the supermind, and the gnostic being, Aurobindo had no inclination to listen to or learn from most people who were themselves unaware of these realities; on the contrary, he was attempting to speak to them of his own supramental vision and divine understandings. Placing the issue in this context, Aurobindo's comments locate his questioner/critic in the disadvantageous position of being on the outside of a revelatory experience. Without such experience one's criticisms of it cannot be taken seriously.

From within the experience, Aurobindo assures us that his reading of his experiences is not without discriminating testing procedures. But they are procedures unfamiliar to those who do not enjoy or do not recognize the uniqueness of such spiritual experience. For this reason Varma's observation is undoubtedly accurate: because Aurobindo's emphasis is on mystic-yogic experience, he will most likely never be able to gain universal empathy or acceptance.[15] Yet, for some, such an experiential base will be a strength. As Eliot Deutsch words it, because Aurobindo's metaphysic is based on spiritual experience, it "is an art more than a science" and its "power lies not in explaining the world but in evoking an experience of it."[16]

Since Aurobindo states that he and the Mother share the same consciousness,[17] it is pertinent to cite a passage from her teachings at this point in order to shed still further light on Aurobindo's understanding of the distinction in planes of consciousness as well as his theory of freedom. In conversation in 1931 the Mother distinguished the plane of divine consciousness from the plane of the lower level of consciousness. On the plane of divine consciousness

all is known absolutely, and the whole plan of things foreseen and predetermined . . . . But when we do not possess that consciousness, it is useless to speak in terms that hold good only in that region and are not our present effective way of seeing things. For at a lower level of consciousness nothing is realised or fixed beforehand; all is in the process of making.[18]

Having established the relationship between the higher and the lower levels of consciousness, she then describes the implications this has for freedom.

> In the plane of matter and on the level of the ordinary consciousness
> you are bound hand and foot . . . .But it need not be so. You can shift
> your place if you will: . . .By Yoga you leave the mechanical round of
> Nature in which you are an ignorant slave, a helpless and miserable
> tool, and rise into another plane where you become a conscious
> participant and a dynamic agent in the working out of a higher
> Destiny.[19]

Here the language of surrender gives way to the language of identification in oneness with the divine.

At first the language of all things foreseen and predetermined by the divine conveys a striking contrast to the language of freedom as self-dependence and self-determination, which Aurobindo employs to unfold his concept of freedom in the political sphere. But one must continue to remember the radical difference in levels of consciousness and being. Aurobindo offers a vision of the human person as a complex being embodying the surface self of mind, life, and body, and the real self of the soul and spirit. Distinctions between the *relative freedom* of the surface self, which give way to the *spiritual freedom* of the deeper self in discovery of the spirit and contact with the divine, together with the full and *infinite freedom* of the transformed gnostic being are all important nuances for grasping Aurobindo's thought. The emphasis on self-dependence, independence, and self-determination in Aurobindo's early writings is intended as a corrective to dependence on Britain, which the oppressed Indians needed to hear. Yet even then, deep within Aurobindo's view, the point of such trust in the self was to create an atmosphere in which the inner being of India—the divinity within—might emerge. Self-dependence and self-determination are not ends in themselves, but necessary steps in the larger process of discovering the divine in the world through surrender in yoga. This theme, as we have seen, is explored fully in the later writings, and gives rise to a new language of surrender and control, but with meanings vastly different from the early period. Surrender to and control by the British is an evil to be fought; surrender to and control by the Supermind is the suprarational good to be sought.

This emphasis on surrender however, gives rise to a second difficulty and raises further questions. Does the emphasis on surrender imply a devaluation of the presence of personal power in the individual at the current stage in the evolution? Where such power is recognized, is it viewed as a potential for creativity, as a strength to be encouraged and fostered? Or is it seen as a limitation rooted in involvement in "the Ignorance" to be overcome through surrender in yoga? What are the practical implications of Aurobindo's theory of spiritual evolution? (Does his theory lead one away from real commitment to social needs in the here and now through a desire to enter the movement of the future? Or does he offer a social ethic as well as a supramental supraethic?) To answer these questions is to address the second purpose of this study, namely, to examine the nature of the relationship between the political and spiritual dimensions in Aurobindo's life and thought.

The Relationship between the Political and the Spiritual

Several scholars have commented on this relationship. Beatrice Bruteau observes that "for Aurobindo political life and spiritual life were one."[20] Haridas Chaudhuri writes that Aurobindo's concept of the supermind "shows him the full integration of the social, economic, political, scientific, and technological values of life on the one hand and the esthetic, psychological, ethico-religious, and ontological values of existence on the other."[21] These observations invite further reflection and clarification. In what way are the political and the spiritual "one"? In what way can we speak of the "full integration" of these values? Furthermore, Robert McDermott speaks of a "complementarity of politics and spirituality" that "typifies Sri Aurobindo's ability to draw diverse strains into a rich and dynamic synthesis" in which "he combined politics and Yoga."[22] Such a statement raises questions regarding the meanings of such a "complementarity," and "dynamic synthesis," and urges us to discover more precisely the way in which the political and spiritual were "combined." McDermott also writes: "more than any other figure of modern India, Sri Aurobindo dramatically exemplifies the ideal blending of social-political activism and spiritual discipline."[23]

If this is so, in what way does an "ideal blending" of the social-political and the spiritual take expression? Is Aurobindo's understanding of the relationship between political and spiritual freedom a relationship of ongoing integral union? That is to say, are the political and the spiritual realms reciprocally necessary for completeness? Or is the relationship one of temporal juxtaposition alone?

Aurobindo's letters indicate that he did believe in the possibility of an integral unity between the political sphere and the spiritual sphere. When he began the practice of yoga during his political period, he experienced no opposition[24] and claims to have directed his yogic powers toward effecting political purposes regarding liberation.[25] Furthermore, Aurobindo's letter to Joseph Baptista in 1920 explains that he had always placed a dominant stress on the spiritual dimension of life but that this emphasis was in no way intended to suggest "withdrawal," "contempt," or "disgust" for secular life, and that "all human activity" was "to be included in a complete spiritual life."[26]

But as he progressed in his concentration and meditation the tension between yoga and political concerns gained momentum. In 1932 he indicated that politics had clearly become a distraction from and obstruction to his yogic pursuits: completely cutting his connection with politics he had retired to Pondicherry in order not to have anything "interfere with" his yoga.[27] Sisirkumar Mitra claims that this separation continued throughout his time at Pondicherry: "for the sake of his spiritual work he kept his Ashram also free from all political action."[28] Furthermore, we noted earlier that in conversation with Purani, Aurobindo faulted Gandhi for applying to "ordinary life" what belongs to "spirituality," implying a dissonance between the two realms. Experientially Aurobindo was unable to unite the political and spiritual realms in a way that he had once hoped.

Theoretically, Aurobindo handles the conflict between these two realms as he consistently handles conflict, by casting the apparent opposites into a larger unifying concept.[29] In this case the concept is spiritual evolution, which functions to unify both political and spiritual freedom by accepting political freedom as a rudimentary stage in the total span of time, with spiritual freedom (ulitmately transcendent, infinite freedom) as the fulfilling and completing stage of the process. Both are absorbed into the continuum of time.

But the political arena Aurobindo had known and the political freedom for which he had fought through revolution remain on the lower levels, bound by the ignorance of which they are a part. Talk of "spiritualising politics" provoked Aurobindo to predict that at most such a trend could result in "some kind of Indianised Bolshevism." And though he would not stop anyone inclined to engage in a pro-political attitude and work style, his own posture was that of critic:

> Even to that kind of work I have no objection. Let each man do according to his inspiration. But that is not the real thing. If one pours the spiritual power into all these impure forms,—the water of the Causal ocean into raw vessels—either that raw thing will break and the water be split and lost or the spiritual power will evaporate and only the impure form remain.[30]

To direct one's spiritual concentration and energies into the political sphere is to lose them or dissolve them. The pure (the spiritual) cannot be held by the impure (the political).

Since the concept of spiritual evolution does not value revolution as a continuing phenomenon but seeks to transform it by the higher levels of being and consciousness, it functions to bring humankind beyond struggle, beyond conflict, beyond political needs. Even the ideal of unity to which humanity is moving, as described in *The Human Cycle* and *The Ideal of Human Unity*, is an ideal beyond political needs, a spiritualized world union eventually expressing the supramental level of gnostic divine existence. For this reason it is understandable that the social scientist reading Aurobindo's theory of the relationship between individual and society would feel discontented. Aurobindo does not attempt to buttress his politico-philosophical generalizations with detailed and documented empirical evidence; his intent is to sketch possibilities not yet realized.[31]

Aurobindo's conceptual position regarding the relationship between the political and the spiritual then is this: as the self-dependent (politically free) individual explores the depths of his own self, he becomes the Self-dependent (spiritually free) individual who recognizes that his real self is one with the divine self, on whom he is dependent and by whom he is determined. Eventually, as the gnostic (infinitely free) being, one with the divine in nature and consciousness, he becomes with the divine the determining (no longer determined) force.

In life Aurobindo's experience of these two realms underwent a development. In the early days his spiritual sensitivities functioned as meaning-giving principles and motivating forces for his political activities, and his yogic practices were directed toward gaining political power for the sake of liberation.[32] In this sense Bruteau's comment is accurate. In the early days Aurobindo sensed a oneness between his political and yogic involvements. The movement to Pondicherry, however, reflects a marked change in this relationship.

Although at Pondicherry Aurobindo described the gnostic being as one who could freely accept "the whole of material Nature" in contrast to the normal expectation of "rejection" and "refusal,"[33] Aurobindo's own life-style (as his biographers tell us) became one of less and less availability to people as his years continued. The decisions to make public his opposition to Hitler and his support of the Cripps proposal were exceptions to this move toward withdrawal; but since Aurobindo was not supported on the Cripps issue, the experience only reinforced his earlier decision to retire from the public forum. The fact that there are no politics allowed at the Sri Aurobindo Ashram suggests that the Mother too saw politics as peripheral to and even in conflict with the practice of yoga, though it is expected that in the long run integral yoga will have an impact on the sociohistorical dimension of human life.

From the point of view of the current movement of evolution, Aurobindo's thought as well as his life indicates that the weakness of the political dimension is that it detracts from and distracts from the intensity of spiritual growth. And while from the point of view of the goal of spiritual evolution it is legitimate to say that Aurobindo's thought integrates the spiritual and the material into a vision of life that is completed by the harmony of physical existence and spiritual existence, this is not the same as saying that his thought integrates the political and the spiritual.

Aurobindo's use of the term *integral* is made with reference to the quality of his yoga, not with reference to the relationship between yoga and politics. He teaches that his yoga is integral because it is based on a spiritual and even supramental transformation of matter rather than escape from matter.[34] This is to say that there is a turning of the entire being in all its parts, body, mind, spirit (not simply the spirit alone) to the divine. It means that the descent of the divine is an intrinsic element in the yoga as the completion of the being's ascent to the divine. This descent of the divine permeates the being and thus transforms that being into its own divine nature.[35] Aurobindo remarks that, whereas "Buddha and Shankara supposed the world to be radically false and miserable" and "therefore escape from the world was to them the only wisdom,"[36] for him "this world is Brahman, the world is God."[37] The world is the unfolding and the movement of God in his own being.[38]

The quality of integralness is that it does not reject nor repudiate matter but absorbs it into its own evolutionary momentum toward the fullest expression of the spirit, the supermind. This supramental existence is trans-ethical, trans-legal, transcendent to the political realm without any truly integral connection with it. The political realm may be preliminary to and preparatory for the spiritual realm in the history of an individual as in the life of Aurobindo himself. But since conflict, struggle, and compromise are at the heart of the political forum, and since Aurobindo encourages a spiritually based life oriented toward the (conflictless) supramental existence, it is inaccurate and misleading to assert that for him the political and the spiritual spheres become integrally united or synthesized. Though the political and the spiritual are "combined" in Aurobindo's concern and in his life, and though the *struggle* to synthesize apparent opposites pervades his work at every point, the texts indicate that he never achieved a "full integration" nor "dynamic synthesis" between the political and the spiritual. In his early (political) period, such a synthesis seemed desirable, for Aurobindo valued both political involvement and yogic commitment and he wished to justify and harmonize both concerns. But in the later (spiritual) period, to integrate the two was no longer necessary, for Aurobindo no longer viewed political involvement as a value to be nourished. His vision of the supramental provoked him to devalue the political forum as an "impure form" unworthy of one's energy. To say that Aurobindo dramatically exemplifies an "ideal blending of social-political activism and spiritual discipline" at most refers to chronological sequence, not to matured philosophical conviction nor intended contribution.

Because Aurobindo does not really value involvement in the practicalities of the sociopolitical present as a necessary element in the growth to supermind, he does not offer a social ethic integral to his ethic of spirituality and eventual supraethic of supramental existence. That is to say, he does not urge his followers to spend their energies fighting social evils such as hunger, poverty, repression and corruption in government, and the like. For Aurobindo grew into the conviction ''that man can never get out of the futile circle the race is always treading until he has raised himself on to the new foundation.''[39] Thus, he urges his followers to seek that new foundation, which is a new consciousness rooted in the spiritual. Such a pursuit seriously and sincerely engaged in will bring about the individual's transformation and will serve as invitation and model of hope to others. Eventually, when the evolutionary ascent to supermind is made, the descent of supermind to material existence follows. But this is no longer the political sphere. It is a supramental sphere beyond political problems, in which the ideal of humanity becomes historically real.

This lack of a social ethic invites conjecture regarding Aurobindo's impact on the future of religiosocial reform in India. Nineteenth- and twentieth-century social reform movements such as the Brāhmo Samāj, the Ārya Samāj, the Ramakrishna Movement, the Nationalist Movement, Gandhi's initiatives, and Vinoba Bhave's land-grant campaign have given a fresh impetus to modern India, shifting its focus from a preoccupation with the Absolute to concern with problems in the social order.

Since many of these reformers have come from Bengal, a saying is reported to have arisen: ''what Bengal does today, all India will do tomorrow.''[40] If there is any truth to this saying, we might well wonder if the choices made by Aurobindo and the many Bengalese who comprise the ashram do indicate the direction of the country in the future. Again, Aurobindo's own words invite quotation: ''The value of our actions lies not so much in their apparent nature and outward result as in their help towards the growth of the Divine within us.''[41] In the light of this his perspective, another question emerges: is it possible that Aurobindo's impact might delay or even impede the progress of social reform in India? Studies on the contribution and impact of the Mother and of the communities at Auroville and at the Ashram need to be made in any attempt to answer such a question. Hopefully, results from such research will be available before long.

Summary

Aurobindo has contributed an understanding of freedom that speaks to both the public concern for political liberation and the more personal search for freedom of the spirit, individually and communally considered. For both he provides a frame of reference that is religious. Political freedom is further focused within a framework of *revolution*, whereas spiritual freedom is cast into the contour of *evolution*. The goal of revolution is independence; the hope of evolution is surrender to the divine. The laws of nature disclose humanity's most radical instincts for growth as expressed in liberty as well as equality and fraternity. These aspirations lie within the human experience, where they are identified with the law of the divine within.

The strengths of his contribution are many. Aurobindo possesses a magnificent command of the English language and his words enable us to hear the yearnings and feel the rebellion of a people exploited and manipulated by a foreign presence. He exhibits an inspiring trust in the possibilities of his people's growth, indicating his conviction that they have much to teach the West about life's deepest values. Aurobindo's divine-law/natural-law identification provides a point of contact for both theist and humanist, enabling both to hear him out and to learn together about the meaning of human life. As political activist, Aurobindo offers a keen sense of judgment, consciously weighing the elements of human tolerance for injustice together with the efficacy of armed revolt and/or passive resistance. His theory of freedom accounts for the curious combination of both freedom and determinism, grounded as it is within experience itself. And his concept of spiritual evolution provides a horizon of meaning that accounts for an awareness of the multifariousness of reality—as material and spiritual, individual and communal, immanent and transcendent. The recommendations he offers for the attainment of political and spiritual freedom are consistent with his metaphysical worldview.

Yet the difficulties discovered cannot be denied. Problems that emerge need to be pressed as research continues, and as the differences in experience, presupposition, and linguistic connotation become more clearly recognized. Admittedly Aurobindo's hope is to create a new alternative for harmonious living by accelerating the evolutionary process through the practice of yoga; he is not interested in perpetuating piecemeal and patchwork efforts, which too often characterize political plans for improvement. Yet, from my point of view, Aurobindo's valuation of yogic surrender runs the risk of devaluing sociopolitical responsibility in the face of evil during this current stage in the evolutionary process.

In assessing Aurobindo's contribution to our experience and ideal of freedom both politically and spiritually, it is important to be clear about the nature of the relationship—or lack of it—between the political and the spiritual. Aurobindo combines them in a life history that is marked by political leadership and heightened spiritual consciousness. But his writings make it evident that as his spiritual sensitivities developed into a more intense consciousness of the divine, the role of the political sphere receded in significance. Ultimately, he handles political realities by cutting connections, ignoring, or, at best, tolerating them.[42] But the political field is never embraced, because the problems it proffers, the conflicts it contains, and the decisions it demands are left behind in the ascent to an ideal of human society characterized by perfection in place of problems, harmony without conflict.

Aurobindo's thought is shot through with a hopeful vision of human possibilities inviting us to consider a future marked with both freedom and unity rooted in a consciousness of and surrender to the spirit. Although his contribution to thought and experience evokes question as well as admiration, to be in touch with his writings is to be richer for the contact and to intend that it continue.

Notes

1. ''Religious Revolutionaries of the Third World: Gandhi, Gandhians, and *Guerrilleros*,'' in *The Meanings of Gandhi*, ed. Paul F. Power (Hawaii: University Press, East-West Center, 1971), pp. 135-52.

2. Arthur Waskow, Jewish radical and radical Jew, comments on this shift also in *The Bush Is Burning! Radical Judaism Faces the Pharaohs of the Modern Superstate* (New York: Macmillan, 1971), pp. 14-15: ''When I started looking carefully at the 'religious question,' it became clear that something remarkable was happening among young Americans. Religion has become not only an arena of insurgency but a *form* of insurgency . . . .Precisely on the Left, where for a century the automatic dogma had been that religion was the opiate of the people, religion had been turned from a narcotic into an awakener.''
James Cone adopts this position also in *A Black Theology of Liberation* (New York: Lippincott, 1970), where he grounds the ''Blackamerican'' struggle within the context of Christian theology.

3. *Aurobindo Ghose*, pp. 140-48.

4. It is in terms of these human rights as well as Vedic references that we find

Aurobindo pointing to the injustice of the *modern* forms of the caste system. Aurobindo did not spend his energies fighting for internal social freedoms because he felt that the more urgent issue was political freedom from external control, but in both the speeches and essays, he did voice criticisms of the way the caste system had become a vehicle for injustice in recent times.

5. "The Thorough Revolutionary," in Peter L. Berger and Richard J. Neuhaus, *Movement and Revolution* (Garden City, N.Y.: Doubleday, 1970), p. 161.

6. Selected writings of Gandhi: *An Autobiography: The Story of My Experiments with Truth* (Boston: Beacon, 1970); *The Gospel of Selfless Action or The Gita According to Gandhi*, ed. Mahadev Desai (Ahmedabad: Navajivan, 1951); *Hind Swaraj or Indian Home Rule* (Ahmedabad: Navajivan, n.d.); *Non-Violent Resistance (Satyagraha)* (New York: Schocken, 1970); *The Teaching of the Gita* (Bombay: Bharatiya Vidya Bhavan, 1962). Of Martin Luther King: *Stride Toward Freedom: The Montgomery Story* (New York: Harper & Row, 1964); *Where Do We Go From Here? Chaos or Community?* (Boston: Beacon, 1967); *Why We Can't Wait* (New York: New American Library, 1964).

7. P. 187.

8. *Ibid.*, pp. 249-50.

9. *Pedagogy of the Oppressed*, trans. Myra Bergman Ramos (New York: Herder and Herder, 1972).

10. *Ibid.*, p. 42.

11. *Ibid.*, p. 52.

12. *Karmayogin*, 2: 61-62, 25.

13. *On Himself*, 26: 91-92.

14. *Ibid.*, p. 92.

15. *Political Philosophy*, p. 130.

16. "Sri Aurobindo's Interpretation of Spiritual Experience: A Critique," *International Philosophical Quarterly* 4, no. 4 (December 1964): 593. See also J. Bruce Long's critically provocative essay, "A New Yoga for a New Age: A Critical Introduction to THE SYNTHESIS OF YOGA," in *Six Pillars*, ed. McDermott, pp. 97-128.

17. *On Himself*, 26: 455.

18. *Conversations* (Pondicherry: Sri Aurobindo Ashram, 1971), p. 34.

19. *Ibid.*, pp. 35-36.

20. *World*, p. 25.

21. "The Supermind in Sri Aurobindo's Philosophy," *International Philosophical Quarterly* 12, no. 2 (June 1972): 181.

22. Introduction to *The Mind of Light* (New York: Dutton, 1971), p. 9.

23. "Editor's Introduction: Vision of a Transformed World" in *The Essential Aurobindo*, p. 3.

24. *On Himself*, 26: 50-51.

25. Purani, *Life*, p. 120.

26. *On Himself*, 26: 430.

27. *Ibid.*, p. 55.

28. S. K. Mitra, *Sri Aurobindo and Indian Freedom* (Madras: Sri Aurobindo Library, 1948), p. 67.

29. Examples include the conflict between nationalism and internationalism, which Aurobindo resolves in the notion of India's mission to the world; the gap between matter and spirit is overcome within the framework of spiritual evolution; the split between good and evil is handled by seeing evil as disguised good; the best elements of the various historical types of society are incorporated into his futuristic ideal for humanity. In "Sri Aurobindo as the Fulfillment of Hinduism," *International Philosophical Quarterly* 12, no. 2 (June 1972): 234-42, Jehangir Chubb describes this characteristic of synthesizing opposites as consistent with and the flowering of the best in the Hindu tradition. J. Bruce Long wonders about that ("A New Yoga for a New Age," in *Six Pillars*, ed. McDermott, p. 126).

30. (1920) *Sri Aurobindo Mandir Annual*, no. 26 (August 15, 1967), p. 126.

31. See Varma, *Political Philosophy*, pp. 164, 436-38.

32. In *Mahayogi*, p. 147, Diwakar finds it questionable "whether he would have entered politics at all, if it had not afforded him an opportunity to rouse the spiritual consciousness of the people."

33. *Life Divine*, 19: 986.

34. *On Himself*, 26: 110.

35. *Letters on Yoga*, 23: 525; *Synthesis of Yoga*, 20: 40.

36. *The Hour of God*, 17: 49.

37. *Ibid.*, p. 49.

38. *Ibid.*, p. 50.

39. Letter to C. R. Das, dated November 18, 1922, *On Himself*, 26: 437.

40. Thomas Berry, *Religions of India* (New York: Bruce, 1971), p. 67.

41. *Social and Political Thought*, 15: 143.

42. See nn 27, 28, and 30, this chapter.

Selected Bibliography

Primary Sources

Ghose, Sri Aurobindo. *Sri Aurobindo Birth Centenary Library*. 30 vols.
Pondicherry: Sri Aurobindo Ashram, 1972. Specific volumes
consulted in this study include:
1, *Bande Mataram*: Early Political Writings—1
2, *Karmayogin*: Early Political Writings—2
3, *The Harmony of Virtue*: Early Cultural Writings
13, *Essays on the Gita*
14, *The Foundations of Indian Culture*
15, *Social and Political Thought*
16, *The Supramental Manifestation and Other Writings*
17, *The Hour of God*
18, *The Life Divine* (Book One and Book Two Part One)
19, *The Life Divine* (Book Two Part Two)
20, *The Synthesis of Yoga* (Parts One and Two)
21, *The Synthesis of Yoga* (Parts Three and Four)
22, *Letters on Yoga* (Part One)
23, *Letters on Yoga* (Parts Two and Three)
24, *Letters on Yoga* (Part Four)
25, *The Mother*
26, *On Himself*
27, *Supplement*
30, *Index*

————. *Complete Works of Sri Aurobindo in Bengali rendered into English*, 1, in *Sri Aurobindo Mandir Annual*, no. 26 (August 15, 1967).

————. *Complete Works of Sri Aurobindo in Bengali rendered into English*, 2, in *Sri Aurobindo Mandir Annual*, no. 27, (August 15, 1968).

————. *Dictionary of Sri Aurobindo's Yoga*. Compiled by M. P. Pandit. Pondicherry: Dipti Publications, 1966.

Secondary Sources — Books

Bolle, Kees W. *The Persistence of Religion: An Essay on Tantrism and Sri Aurobindo's Philosophy*. With a preface by Mircea Eliade. Leiden: Brill, 1965.

Bruteau, Beatrice. *Worthy Is the World: The Hindu Philosophy of Sri Aurobindo*. Madison: Fairleigh Dickinson University Press, 1971.

Chaudhuri, Haridas, and Spiegelberg, Frederic, eds. *The Integral Philosophy of Sri Aurobindo: A Commemorative Symposium*. London: Allen & Unwin, 1960.

————. *The Philosophy of Integralism: the Metaphysical Synthesis in Sri Aurobindo's Teaching*. 2nd enl. ed. Pondicherry: Sri Aurobindo Ashram, 1967.

Chincholkar, Laxman Ganpatrao. *A Critical Study of Aurobindo: with Special Reference to his Concept of Spiritual Evolution*. Nagpur, 1966?

Das, Manoj. *Sri Aurobindo in the First Decade of the Century*. Pondicherry: Sri Aurobindo Ashram, 1972.

Diwakar, Ranganath Ramachandra. *Mahayogi Sri Aurobindo: Life, Sadhana and Teachings of Sri Aurobindo*. 3rd rev. enl. ed. Bombay: Bharatiya Vidya Bhavan, 1962.

Donnelly, Morwenna. *Founding the Life Divine: An Introduction to the Integral Yoga of Sri Aurobindo*. London: New York Rider, 1955.

Gandhi, Kishor. *Social Philosophy and the New Age*. Pondicherry: Sri Aurobindo Society, 1965.

Gupta, Nolini Kanta. *A Century's Salutation to Sri Aurobindo*. Pondicherry: Sri Aurobindo Ashram, 1972.

———— and Amrita, K. *Reminiscences*. 1st ed. Pondicherry: Mother India, Sri Aurobindo Ashram, 1969.

————— *et al*., eds. *Sri Aurobindo and His Ashram*. 1st ed. Calcutta: Arya Publishing House, 1948.

—————. *The Yoga of Sri Aurobindo (Parts I to IV)*. Pondicherry: Sri Aurobindo Ashram, 1967.

Iyengar, K. R. Srinivasa. *Sri Aurobindo*. 3rd rev. enl. ed. 2 vols. Pondicherry: Sri Aurobindo Ashram, 1972.

Keshavmurti. *Sri Aurobindo, The Hope of Man*. Pondicherry: Dipti Publications, Sri Aurobindo Ashram, 1969.

Langley, George Harry. *Sri Aurobindo, Indian Poet, Philosopher and Mystic*. London: D. Marlowe for the Royal India and Pakistan Society, 1949.

McDermott, Robert A., ed. *Six Pillars: An Introduction to the Major Works of Sri Aurobindo*. Chambersburg, Pa.: Wilson Books, 1974.

Maitra, Susil Kumar. *An Introduction to the Philosophy of Sri Aurobindo*. 1st ed. Calcutta: The Culture Publishers, 1941.

—————. *The Meeting of the East and the West in Sri Aurobindo's Philosophy*. 1st ed. Pondicherry: Sri Aurobindo Ashram, 1968.

—————. *Studies in Sri Aurobindo's Philosophy*. Benares: Benares Hindu University, 1945.

Mitra, Sisirkumar. *India's Evolution, Its Meaning*. Bombay: Jaico Publishing House, 1968.

—————. *The Liberator: Sri Aurobindo, India and the World*. Rev. ed. Bombay: Jaico Publishing House, 1970.

—————. *Resurgent India*. New York: Allied Publishers, 1963.

—————. *Sri Aurobindo*. New Delhi: Indian Book Company, 1972.

—————. *Sri Aurobindo and Indian Freedom*. Madras: Sri Aurobindo Library, 1948.

Nirodbaran. *Talks with Sri Aurobindo*. vol. 1. Calcutta: Sri Aurobindo Pathamandir, 1966.

Pandit, Madhav Pundalik. *Sadhana in Sri Aurobindo's Yoga*. Pondicherry?, 1962.

Pearson, Nathaniel. *Sri Aurobindo and the Soul-Quest of Man: Three Steps to Spiritual Knowledge (Study of Chapters 1-12 of Life Divine)*. London: G. Allen & Unwin, 1952.

Prasad, Narayan. *Life in Sri Aurobindo Ashram*. Pondicherry: Sri Aurobindo Ashram, 1965.

Purani, Ambalal Balkrishna. *Evening Talks with Sri Aurobindo*. 1st ser. 2nd ed. Pondicherry: Sri Aurobindo Ashram Trust, 1970.

————. *The Life of Sri Aurobindo (1872-1926)*. 2nd ed. Pondicherry: Sri Aurobindo Ashram, 1960.

————. *Sri Aurobindo: Some Aspects of His Vision*. 1st ed. Bombay: Bharatiya Vidya Bhavan, 1966.

————. *Sri Aurobindo's Life Divine: Lectures Delivered in the USA*. 1st ed. Pondicherry: Sri Aurobindo Ashram, 1966.

Reddy, V. Madhusudan. *Sri Aurobindo's Philosophy of Evolution*. Hyderabad: Institute of Human Study, 1966.

Roy, Anilbaran. *Sri Aurobindo and the New Age*. 2nd ed. Pondicherry: Divyajivan Sahitya Prakashan, available from Gita Prachar Karyalaya, Calcutta, 1965.

Roy, Dilip Kumar. *Among the Great: Conversations with Sri Aurobindo and Others*. With an introduction by Sri S. Radhakrishnan. Bombay: Jaico Publishing House, 1950.

————. *Sri Aurobindo Came to Me: Reminiscences*. 2nd ed. Bombay: Jaico Publishing House, 1964.

Satprem. *Sri Aurobindo or the Adventure of Consciousness*. Pondicherry: Sri Aurobindo Ashram, 1970.

Sethna, Kaikhushur Dhunkibhoy. *The Vision and Work of Sri Aurobindo*. Pondicherry: Mother India, 1968.

Sharma, Ram Nath. *The Philosophy of Sri Aurobindo*. 2nd ed. Meerut: Kedar Nath Ram Nath, 1963.

Singh, Herbert Jai. *Sri Aurobindo: His Life and Religious Thought*. Bangalore: Christian Institute for the Study of Religion and Society, 1962.

Singh, Karan. *Prophet of Indian Nationalism: A Study of the Political Thought of Sri Aurobindo Ghosh 1893-1910*. London: George Allen & Unwin, 1963.

Subbannachar, N. V. Social Psychology, the Integral Approach. Calcutta: Scientific Book Agency, 1966.

Varma, Vishwanath Prasad. *The Political Philosophy of Sri Aurobindo*. New York: Asia Publishing House, 1960.

Articles

Bazemore, Duncan. "Life as Battlefield: A Gita Symbol as Interpreted by Sri Aurobindo." *International Philosophical Quarterly* 12, no. 2 (June 1972): 251-59.

Bruteau, Beatrice. "Sri Aurobindo and Teilhard de Chardin on the Problem of Action." *International Philosophical Quarterly* 12, no. 2 (June 1972): 193-204.

Cairns, Grace E. "Aurobindo's Conception of the Nature and Meaning of History." *International Philosophical Quarterly* 12, no. 2 (June 1972): 205-19.

Chakravarti, P.C. "Genesis of the Partition of Bengal (1905)." *The Modern Review* (April 1959), pp. 296-98.

Chaudhuri, Haridas. "The Philosophy and Yoga of Sri Aurobindo." *Philosophy East and West* 22, no. 1 (January 1972): 5-14.

———. "The Supermind in Sri Aurobindo's Philosophy." *International Philosophical Quarterly* 12, no. 2 (June 1972): 181-92.

Chubb, Jehangir N. "Sri Aurobindo as the Fulfillment of Hinduism." *International Philosophical Quarterly* 12, no. 2 (June 1972): 234-42.

Deutsch, Eliot. "Sri Aurobindo's Interpretation of Spiritual Experience: A Critique." *International Philosophical Quarterly* 4, no. 4 (December 1964): 581-94.

Johnson, David L. "The Task of Relevance: Aurobindo's Synthesis of Religion and Politics." *Philosophy East and West* 23, no. 4 (October 1973): 507-15.

Koller, John M. "Types of Society: The Social Thought of Sri Aurobindo." *International Philosophical Quarterly* 12, no. 2 (June 1972): 220-33.

McDermott, Robert A. "The Experiential Basis of Sri Aurobindo's Integral Yoga." *Philosophy East and West* 22, no. 1 (January 1972): 15-23.

———. "Introduction" to *The Mind of Light*. New York: E. P. Dutton, 1971.

———. "The Legacy of Sri Aurobindo." *Cross Currents* 22, no. 1 (Winter 1972): 2-8.

———. "Sri Aurobindo: An Integrated Theory of Individual and Historical Transformation." *International Philosophical Quarterly* 12, no. 2 (June 1972): 168-80.

Index

148